E

EARLY GREEK
PHILOSOPHY

First Edition 1908
Alfred William Benn, B.A.

New Edition 2021
Edited by Tarl Warwick

COPYRIGHT AND DISCLAIMER

FOREWORD

This little work is part of a very long-term series of several dozen texts written over the course of several decades at the end of the 19th and beginning of the 20th centuries, specifically meant to be short, easily digested works for people interested in knowing some basic things about subjects which most often involved ancient religion, folklore, or philosophy. This particular entry is rather well made, albeit somewhat dense, and spans the course of Greek philosophy from the period of Thales of Miletus up through Socrates.

This period of only a few centuries saw one of the most dynamic shifts (at least in the region) of religious and philosophical thought. It is the former that causes me to release an edition of this work (the occult, or more broadly, things of a spiritual or supernatural nature, being my personal interest)- we cannot easily separate Greek philosophy from religion, and more than a few philosophers and other figures were killed in the early period on charges of atheism, among other things. The dynamic of the Greek pantheon according to Homer and other figures is detailed herein as well. A short section on atomism as a precursor to modern science is of especial note.

This edition of "Early Greek Philosophy" has been carefully edited for format and content. Care has been taken to retain all original intent and meaning.

EARLY GREEK PHILOSOPHY

FOREWORD TO THE 1908 EDITION

References to authorities, except of the most general kind, are precluded by the plan of the Series to which this Primer belongs. It is, therefore, as well for me to mention that I have gone to the original sources for my materials. The admirable work of Hermann Diels, *Fragmente der Vorsokratiker*, Bd. i., Berlin, 1906, has been most helpful for the prse-Sophistic philosophers.

As regards the interpretation of early Greek philosophy I have found no reason to depart from the views given in my Philosophy of Greece (1898). At the same time I wish it to be understood that, in my opinion, the very scanty information at our disposal permits no more than a conjectural interpretation of what the Greek philosophers from Thales to Socrates really taught. And it is only fit that the beginner should be told as much on his first introduction to the subject. The great thing is that he should become interested enough in these uncertainties to think that the time spent on them has not been thrown away.

A. W. B.

EARLY GREEK PHILOSOPHY

CHAPTER I

THE SCHOOL OF MILETUS

The Meaning of Philosophy.- It is related of an old Greek sage that on being asked to explain what was meant by philosophy he replied: Life is like a public festival. Some go there to buy and sell, others go to compete in the games, but a third class go simply to look on, and these are the best of all. Well, just in the same way most men are born slaves to the pursuit of gain or glory, whereas the philosopher freely devotes himself to the study of truth.

This idea of philosophy as disinterested speculation has been handed down from the Greeks to ourselves, and has even been widely popularized, as common language seems to prove. Any one who shows a great curiosity about things in general, apart from their utility to himself, any student who, like the young Francis Bacon, takes all knowledge for his province, is apt to be called a philosopher; while conversely, he who has gained the reputation of being a philosopher is expected to know everything- not merely everything that is known already but everything that ever will be known, and some things that perhaps cannot be known at all.

Even popular language, however, is dimly conscious of a distinction between the philosopher and the scholar. Broadly speaking, the one is expected to know all about nature, the other is expected to know all about history and literature. Even his warmest admirers would hardly have called Mr. Gladstone a philosopher; while it might have excited some surprise if any recorded deed or word of any human being from the creation down to the most modern times had escaped his notice. On the other hand it seemed quite in character that the typical philosopher, Herbert Spencer, should be rather proud of not knowing the date of something that happened three centuries ago;

and that he should congratulate himself on not having received a classical education.

Among the Greeks also philosophy was associated in a peculiar manner with the study of nature as distinguished from the study of history and literature, which are more the subjects of what we call scholarship and erudition. And this fact explains how the word philosophy itself came into being. Originally all men who were particularly distinguished for the extent of their knowledge- poets among others- went by the name of "wise", although wisdom with us seems more limited to knowing what is useful for the conduct of life than what a Greek meant by Sophia. Now, in a relatively simple state of society, to know all that can be known about literature, history, and human interests generally seems a not impossible or inordinate ambition. It is otherwise with nature. True, the Greeks as compared with ourselves had hardly an idea of the vastness and complexity of the physical universe; still, such acute and sincere observers could not fail to perceive, when they set their minds to it, how infinitely greater is the world of nature than the world of man. And so it came about that those who took nature rather than man for their province disclaimed the title of wise or knowing men, modestly preferring to be called lovers of knowledge or, as we now say, students, which is precisely what is meant by philosophers.

We are told that the first to adopt the name was the celebrated Pythagoras, who is also credited with the definition of philosophy as disinterested speculation, quoted at the beginning of this book. But it seems likely that both the word and the definition belong to a somewhat later age than that in which Pythagoras lived.

Greek Religion. Before philosophy arose, Greek curiosity about the origin and structure of the material universe was satisfied by an elaborate system of mythology. It is still a matter of dispute how religion first began, but it seems to be generally agreed that all the progressive races have passed through a stage in which their gods are conceived as personified natural objects or natural forces. At any rate, that was how the Greeks represented to themselves the beings whom they worshiped. Working, as we may suppose, on a mass of loose and discordant traditions, their poets elaborated the figments of popular religion into a literary scheme of such unfading interest that an acquaintance with Greek mythology has remained part of a liberal education all over the modern Christian world.

It was a unique circumstance in the history of religion that the Greek poets should play such a decisive part in the evolution of theological belief. That the poets were able to exercise this commanding influence over public opinion arose from the absence among the Greeks of a priestly caste or corporation like those which dominated the great Oriental civilizations. Priests as a class abounded, but they were neither united nor powerful. Each particular sanctuary had its priest, claiming special knowledge of the god to whom it belonged, ready to explain how the favor of that particular divinity could be won or his anger appeased, able perhaps also to tell the legend of the sanctuary, the particular circumstances in which the god came to settle at that place. And even in very ancient times Greek armies on a campaign were attended by soothsayers whom the generals consulted in reference to any great calamity or any striking apparition presumed to be of supernatural origin.

But these officials, although habitually treated with great respect, had no more than a personal authority; neither priests nor soothsayers belonged to an order possessing the enormous wealth and political influence of the Babylonian or Egyptian hierocracies, or of the Catholic Church in medieval Europe. Assuming intellectual curiosity and intellectual progress to be good things, it was fortunate for the Greek mind that traditional beliefs had no stronger support than the ordinary conservatism of human nature, that they were not bound up with the material interests of a body accustomed to identify the truth of their opinions about the gods with the preservation of their corporate property.

Greek Mythology in a systematized form was, as I have said, a creation of the poets, and more particularly of Homer and Hesiod. With Hesiod the conception of the gods as nature-powers is quite evident; Homer presents them more as personal beings; but with him also evidence of their purely physical origin and nature is never far to seek. Zeus constantly appears as the cloud-collector, that is, the upper heaven; Athene bears the aegis or cloud-shield of her father Zeus; Apollo, his son, the far-darter, is distinguished by the unmistakable attributes of a solar deity. And there seems to be a latent consciousness, at least in what are supposed to be the more recent portions of the *Iliad*, not only that the Olympian gods are nature-powers but also that they have no existence except as indwelling spirits of nature.

Their detachment from material objects, the conception of them as self-conscious personal beings, is of course most complete when they are brought together in conclave for purposes of deliberation or festivity. Now it is just on those occasions that Homer takes his gods and goddesses least seriously, presenting them even in a ludicrous light, with a certain skeptical irony.

Nature is not moral, and the gods of Greek poetry are neither exhibited as themselves models of good conduct, nor as necessarily encouraging good conduct among mortals. In fact they behave as men and women might be expected to behave if they lived for ever and were clothed with irresistible power. Their life among themselves is that of a dissolute aristocracy; their treatment of the human race is determined by the frankest favoritism. An organized priesthood would not have tolerated such undignified proceedings in the objects of its worship as Homer reports.

At the same time, in default of a priesthood- better even in some ways than a priesthood- public opinion among the Greeks did something to moralize religion. The gods were supposed to govern human affairs; and rulers, whether real or imaginary, cannot but become associated to some extent with ideas of justice. They became more particularly associated with the keeping of promises, which is the very foundation of social order, by the Greek custom of invoking them as witnesses to oaths. For to break an oath which a god had witnessed was, as the Decalogue puts it, taking his name in vain- conduct which he naturally resented. Moreover Zeus, the supreme god, "father of gods and men," was regarded as being in a particular way the patron of destitute persons and of strangers. At the same time it must not be supposed that morality ever became so completely identified with religion in Greece as in ancient Israel or among Christian nations. And to the fact of their distinction is due the constitution of an independent moral philosophy by the early Greek thinkers- perhaps also the constitution of an independent physical philosophy as well.

The Seven Sages. In an early stage of civilization people are saved the trouble of thinking about moral philosophy or abstract principles of right conduct by learning the laws and customs of their land or tribe, just as mythology saves them the trouble of finding scientific explanations of natural processes. But where a number of petty states exist side by side, each with laws of its own, where repeated changes of government involve the necessity of making new laws, above all where the individual members of the community have so far emancipated themselves from the yoke of custom as to exercise a certain discretion in the management of their private affairs, there a sort of moral rationalism will arise, an idea that certain things should be done because they are good in themselves, not because they are prescribed by authority.

These conditions were fulfilled to a remarkable extent in the Hellenic world during the first half of the sixth century B.C. The old patriarchal monarchies, such as we find still existing in Homer's time, had given place to aristocratic republics; and in many instances one of the aristocrats had succeeded for a time in making himself what the Greeks called a tyrant, or absolute ruler, by playing off the people against the nobles. Men who formerly occupied a leading position in their own city were driven into exile and spent their enforced leisure in visiting foreign parts and studying the varieties of human life there offered to their observation. A vast extension of commerce brought the Greek mind into vivifying contact with the great Oriental civilizations and with the uncivilized inhabitants of Northern Europe. Moreover, the economical revolution brought with it unexpected changes of fortune and new valuations of personal worth. It came to be a popular saying that "money makes the man"- long descent counting for little or nothing when the hereditary magnate had lost his paternal estates.

It was in these circumstances that a group of worthies became widely celebrated under the name of the Seven Sages of Greece. Each sage got the credit of having originated some pithy saying which thenceforward became a current coin in the treasure of popular wisdom. What strikes us most about these adages is their brevity and the abstract wording that distinguishes them from the proverbs of other nations. Some of them had the glory of being inscribed on the walls of the temple at Delphi; and two in particular are pregnant with a wisdom that the highest Greek ethical teaching did but expand and apply.

These are, "Be moderate" and "Know thyself." To realize and practice the duties they recommend was to possess in its fullness what was par excellence the Greek virtue of Sophrosyne. We ordinarily render the word by Temperance; but temperance even in the wide sense of avoiding excess in every direction fails to convey its full meaning; for he to whom nature or training has given Sophrosyne adds the faculty of self-knowledge to the faculty of self-control. He is what artists call the master of his means; he has learned what he can do, and does it; something tells him how far he can go; up to that point he goes, but not a step beyond.

Opposed to Sophrosyne as the ideal Greek virtue was what one may call the ideal Greek vice, in the sense of what wise Greeks most abhorred, that is, Hybris. Literally hybris means no more than excess, and some trace of this significance survives in our own word hybrid, used primarily of animals that are a cross between two species, thus as it were exceeding the limits assigned to them by nature. Morally and etymologically hybris is also connected with the word outrage, which literally means no more than "going beyond"- that is, beyond what reason and law prescribe, but which in the evolution of language has come to mean going beyond the bounds of ordinary license and crime. The Greeks as a dignified and self-respecting people were peculiarly sensitive to all such transgressions, from insolent and overbearing language to acts of unprovoked and gross personal violence committed in the mere wantonness of irresistible power. Nature, as they conceived her, is bound by strict laws of limitation; and therefore the gods, being nature-powers, showed themselves particularly hostile to hybris; and the poetic interpretations of mythology all went to show that the old kingly races had perished by drawing down divine vengeance on their parricidal crimes or on their incestuous loves. In historic times the same feeling was particularly directed against the outrageous abuses of power committed by tyrants on the one side and by unbridled democracies on the other. As a mean between these two extremes, aristocracy found most favor with thinking men; while if a democracy had become firmly established, they looked to the middle class as the best guardian of social order against the turbulence of the nobles or of the people.

The Reign of Law. I have said that the Greeks conceived nature as bound by a law of limitation. This conception is so closely connected with their habits of political self-government, with the fact that their cities were constituted as free republics, each jealously guarding its independence against all the others, that we cannot tell which came first, the political organization or the creed. At any rate, that their republican habits led to the philosophical idea of nature as a self-sufficing orderly universe, developed on impersonal lines, undisturbed by the arbitrary volitions of supernatural beings, seems likely An Oriental, brought up on traditions of personal government, could not easily grasp that idea, could not but conceive the material world as subject like himself to the will of an irresponsible master. And even the few self-governing Semitic communities remained subject in religion to priesthoods that preserved the tradition of a celestial autocracy intact. The Greeks, as we saw, had no such priesthood, and therefore their high intelligence was left free to work out a truly scientific philosophy of nature.

In positive science, on the other hand, Greece was much behind the great Oriental theocracies. These had long promoted the study of arithmetic, geometry, and astronomy, although more as adjuncts to magic and religion than from pure speculative curiosity. Such curiosity was, as we have seen, the characteristic note of philosophy; and it is a signal merit of the early Greek thinkers that they should have known how to carry away what was really valuable in Eastern learning while discarding nearly the whole of the superstition in which it was embedded.

Thales. Among the seven sages of Greece, Solon of Athens has remained through all ages the most celebrated for practical genius; and many who would be puzzled to tell when or where he lived have heard of him as an ideally wise man. To those, however, who are not studying the history of politics but the history of thought, the most interesting of the whole band is not Solon but Thales of Miletus, the founder of Greek and indeed of all European philosophy. It is no accident that this wonderful man should have been a Milesian. At the time when he flourished, that is to say, early in the sixth century B.C., Miletus was the most prosperous of the Ionian cities in Asia Minor, and the Ionians stood intellectually at the head of the whole Hellenic race, the furthest removed from primitive barbarism, the least exposed to contagion from the contemporary barbarism that surrounded

EARLY GREEK PHILOSOPHY

Hellas like a sea on every side. We know that religious skepticism began at a comparatively early date among the Ionian Greeks, for those parts of the Homeric poems where the gods are exhibited in a rather ridiculous light, although among the latest additions to the original epic, are still very ancient, and these are evidently the work of an Ionian hand. It only remained to substitute a serious scientific explanation of the world for the discredited Olympian mythology, and this was first attempted in the school of Miletus.

Thales was not a writer of books, and what we know about him comes from reports of which the earliest cannot be dated nearer than half a century after his death, while the most important information of all comes from Aristotle, who lived not much less than two and a half centuries later than his time. But it all seems credible enough; and on putting these scattered notices together we reach the conception of Thales as a true master of those who know, combining great practical sagacity with a firm grasp of scientific realities, so far as they were then accessible, and an instinctive feeling out after that universality which alone can lift positive science to the supreme heights of synthetic philosophy. He is credited with having discovered certain elementary propositions of geometry; that the angles at the base of an isosceles triangle are equal, and that if two straight lines intersect the opposite angles are equal. Any one can see by looking at the figures that the fact is so; perhaps Thales first proved that it must be so. And he is also stated on good authority to have predicted an eclipse of the sun which the calculations of modern astronomy show to have occurred in the year 585 B.C. Apparently Thales owed his place among the Seven Sages to that lucky forecast.

I say lucky, because at that time astronomers knew no more than that eclipses recur at certain intervals; they were unable to tell whether a particular eclipse would be visible on a certain part of the earth's surface or not. Thales, no doubt, ascertained by studying the tables drawn up by Babylonian astrologers that a solar eclipse would be visible somewhere or other that year. By good fortune not only was it visible in Asia Minor but it also fell on the day of a great battle between the Lydians and the Medes, so alarming the combatants that they separated and made peace.

So much for Thales as a man of science. As a philosopher, he taught that water is the principle of all things, or what we should call the fundamental element. It was a Semitic idea, quite familiar to us from the earlier chapters of Genesis, that the earth is surrounded by water on all sides, being protected against an in-flooding of the great deep below by its own solid structure, and against irruptions from above by the solid vault of heaven- a notion whence our word "firmament" is derived. In like manner modern science conceives the earth and all the heavenly bodies as surrounded by a vast sea of ether, the medium by whose pulsations light, heat, electricity, and perhaps even gravitation are constituted and transmitted.

Now the idea has been gaining ground for some years past that matter is made out of ether, was originally evolved from ethereal particles or pulses, and is perhaps destined to resolve itself into them again. And it would seem that Thales came to the same conclusion about the derivation of all things from water by a more summary process than modern science would approve of, but in a spirit closely akin to that of our own most advanced physical investigators, the generalizing, assimilating spirit so characteristic of philosophy in every age. Another recorded saying of the Milesian pioneer points in the same direction: "All things are full of gods." Here, at first sight, we seem to have the old mythology back again, to be no further advanced than Hesiod was when he represented the great cosmic powers as personal beings, marrying, begetting children, and quarreling with one another. If, however, we take the words in connection with the general drift of his teaching, they acquire another meaning. Had the citizens of a Greek republic been addressed as so many kings they would none the less have represented a realm of law and order as against the personal despotisms of the East; and so, when Thales said that there was a god in amber or a god in the lodestone, he really meant that the drifting cloud and the falling thunderbolt belonged to the same world of natural occurrences as the phenomena, then first beginning to be scientifically observed, of magnetism and electricity.

Anaximander. I have said that Thales probably learned what astronomy he knew from Babylon, and that his view of the relation between earth and water was Semitic. Now it is certain that the philosopher was not of pure Greek race; and one rather doubtful pedigree even makes him belong to a Phoenician, that is to say, a Semitic family. There seem to be very insufficient grounds for the belief; but were it true, philosophy would remain a product of European not of Asiatic culture, while the fertilizing stimulus that first started Greek thought seems to have come not from any Semitic source but from Egypt. At any rate the beginnings of speculation at Miletus coincide with the permanent establishment of a Milesian colony at Naucratis in the Delta, a concession due to the liberality of the very enlightened Pharaoh, Amasis.

With Anaximander, the pupil of Thales, and like him a Milesian (born 610 B.C.), we already stand on more solid ground. This marvelous thinker may be caviled the second founder of philosophy, for he first gave it literary expression in a book of which some fragments still survive. According to him the primary substance whence all things arise is not water, nor, indeed, any form of matter known to us, but an infinite something without limit in space or time. Out of this all the worlds are evolved by a necessary process of succession, and into it they return when their fated term of existence is completed. Only so, as Anaximander thinks, can the eternal laws of justice be fulfilled. No single combination of material conditions among the boundless possibilities of existence has a right to continue forever, blocking the way that others also are waiting to traverse in their turn. Here we have the cardinal Greek virtue of Sophrosyne, the Ionian rule of self-limitation, raised to the dignity of a universal law, determining the life and death of things in themselves.

There is no room in Anaximander's system for the immortal gods of Homer; each world in the infinite succession of worlds is a god indeed, but a god destined to perish like ourselves. Like Thales, Anaximander has a place in the history of science no less than in the history of philosophy- perhaps even a greater place. We are told that he made the first map; and that he conceived the earth as hanging unsupported in space, although he did not conceive it as a globe but as a cylinder. This, however, marks a considerable advance on his master's view of the earth as a flat disk floating on the water. According to him the heavenly bodies are vast revolving hoops of fire pierced with circular apertures which give us the notion of them as luminous disks. And he anticipated the nebular hypothesis so far as to teach that these hoops were evolved out of the formless Infinite by a process of gradual differentiation.

Evolution was an idea familiar to all the early Greek philosophers. It presents, indeed, no difficulties to men at a much more primitive stage of thought than theirs. We ourselves have grown up gradually from very small beginnings, and the natural thing is to conceive the world as having been developed in the same fashion. Moreover, primitive folk are accustomed to look on the transformation of men into animals or plants, and of animals or plants into men, as quite an ordinary occurrence. It is not, therefore, surprising to find Anaximander saying that land animals were originally developed from aquatic or fishlike animals, and that "man was born from animals of a different species." The remarkable thing is the reason he gives for his theory. "While other animals quickly find food for themselves, man alone requires a prolonged period of suckling. Hence had he been originally such as he is now, he could never have survived."

Anaximenes. We shall see presently what causes brought

the genuinely scientific movement of the Milesian school to an end. Before expiring it produced one more great representative in Anaximenes, the successor of Anaximander. With less speculative daring, he seems to show a closer observation of fact. For him also there is a primal substance of infinite extent, in which and from which all finite things have their being. That elementary substance is Air, the air that we breathe, our very life. To use his own words, "that which is our soul and constitutive principle, also holds the universe together." A philosopher who so expressed himself now, or indeed at any time after Plato, would be properly called a materialist. But we can hardly apply the name to Anaximenes. Materialism and spiritualism are a correlated couple. Each term first becomes intelligible as the antithesis and contradiction of the other.

We have better grounds for crediting Anaximenes with what would now be called a mechanical theory of nature, as distinguished from what, by another modernism, may be described as the "specific energies" or "occult qualities" of his predecessor. Anaximander taught that such antithetical pairs as wet and dry, hot and cold, etc., were separated out or "differentiated" from the homogeneous Infinite where they had previously existed in a latent state. To Anaximenes, on the other hand, heat and cold, like the solid, liquid, and gaseous states of matter, were all merely so many products of rarefaction and condensation. Air squeezed together became cloudy vapor, under additional pressure vapor turned to rain, and rain by the same process to vegetable and animal substances, which ultimately pass into air again. Observing with perfect accuracy that heat and cold are somehow connected with dilatation and compression, this early precursor of Bacon unfortunately reversed the real relation by supposing that air is chilled by being condensed and warmed by being expanded. And that is why, says Anaximenes, we press our lips together when we want to blow cold, and open them when we want to blow hot. In studying the errors of such a man we must remember that to ask questions and answer them wrongly helps progress incomparably more than not to ask them at all.

Good care is taken, says a German proverb, that the trees shall not grow into the sky. Milesian philosophy, with its splendid promise of positive knowledge, perished after the third generation, first choked by rank undergrowths of superstition, then uprooted by earthquake and storm. But the same causes that put an end to speculation in one part of Hellas favored its rise and propagation from new centers of intelligence elsewhere. It was just this multiplication of intellectual centers, leading to the cross-fertilization of mental growths, that gave the Greek genius such an extraordinary productivity, a productivity of which the world's history affords no second example.

CHAPTER II

THE FIRST METAPHYSICIANS

The Religious Revival. In all times and countries the philosophy of a nation has been intimately related to its religious beliefs. And if this is true of modern European thought which has Greek thought to build on as an independent foundation, much more is it true of the original Greek thought which started without any such inheritance from the past. Now it is a remarkable fact that Greek philosophy as it goes on evolving seems to come into closer and closer connection with popular religious belief, with the current pagan theology. Among ourselves, as is well known, rather the reverse process obtains. Since the Middle Ages speculation has tended on the whole to break away from dogmatic trammels. Fully to set out the causes of what seems to us so singular an inversion of the natural order would require a volume; and indeed the problem is one that classical scholarship has not yet completely elucidated; but a few summary indications will be found helpful for the intelligence of what is to follow.

The Greeks had not one religion but two religions; or rather they had many religions, the objects of which grouped themselves under two general headings, according as their home was in the heavens or under the earth. We speak of the one class as Olympian, of the other class as Chthonian deities. The Olympian gods- typified above all by the great triad, Zeus, Apollo, and Athena- are associated in a peculiar way with the bright upper sky and the sun; apart from their human interests they enjoy unchanging and immortal felicity. The Chthonian gods are associated in the first instance with the dead, and their shadowy chief, Pluto, exists only as a personification of the grave; but they are also conceived in a more concrete way as powers of vegetation and growth, of what is sent up from the underworld to the earth's surface, whether plants or springing waters; and these find their most characteristic representatives in Demeter (literally Mother Earth), her daughter Persephone, and Dionysus, originally a god of all subterranean springs, but tending to become specialized as a wine-god.

From their great prominence in Greek classic literature, the Olympian gods have come to figure in our imagination as the proper objects of Greek worship and the centers of Greek religious belief. It seems likely that the religion of the higher classes, whose thoughts and feelings classic literature above all expresses, was in fact Olympian, turning itself by preference to the bright and immortal aspects of nature. On the other hand it was to be expected that the vast laboring population, whose interests lay especially in agriculture, should turn by preference to the Chthonian gods, to the givers of corn, and wine, and oil. These too were more human, more sympathetic than the Olympians in that they shared man's mortality and grief. Every year Demeter, the Earth goddess, mourns for her daughter Persephone, the flower-crowned spring, carried off by the King of Death to share his subterranean throne. Every year Dionysus, the vine-god, gives his body to be torn to pieces and mangled by the vintage and the wine-press. Nor did the process of assimilation end here. From the idea of a dying god came forth the idea of an undying life for man. Persephone returns to her mother every spring in a resurrection of leaves and flowers. And by a still more significant symbolism Dionysus, the twice-born, first from the fruitful vine, then from the wine vat, celebrates a joyful immortality in that life-giving draught which gladdens the hearts of gods and men. Thus for mortal men also the grave came to be thought of as the gateway to another existence- though not necessarily to an existence of everlasting joy. For as it is the very law of life that death should be dreaded, if we cease to fear death as the end of all our happiness here we must learn to fear it as opening the possibility of endless unhappiness hereafter.

It is an economic law that morality should be more prized

and more practiced among the lower than among the higher classes of society. For justice is the appeal of the poor against the tyranny of the rich, and temperance is the guardian of the poor against the vicious self indulgence and extravagance which are so much more speedily fatal to them than to the rich. Hence we find a distinctly more moral tone in Hesiod, who addressed himself to the hardworking rural population, than in Homer, who addressed himself to the idle and warlike aristocracy. Thus when a belief in human immortality came to be developed out of the Chthonian religion it was utilized by the superior moral feeling of the industrial classes as an additional sanction for the laws of right and wrong. A state of future rewards and punishments is unknown to the authors of the Iliad, but we find a scheme of retributive justice after death set out in what critics suppose to be a late addition to the Odyssey.

It is a common experience to find the belief in another world utilized by a particular class to further their own interests by working on the superstitious imagination of the vulgar; and such seems to have been also the case in Greece. An elaborate system of ritualistic observances took the place of righteous conduct as a passport to the dwellings of the blessed; and bloody sacrifices came into high repute as a means for expiating real or imaginary guilt. Such phenomena as Revivalism and Salvationism were not without their counterpart in old Hellas; only there the first stimulus to these tumultuous manifestations of religious feeling seems to have been imported from among the barbarous Thracians or from the rot-heaps of decaying Semitic civilization. Two general causes, subsequently reinforced by a third, operated in the sixth century B.C. to set on foot a great religious movement, beginning with the lower strata of Greek society and spreading upward till it absorbed the highest. A great wave of Asiatic conquest, started long before, but only becoming formidable to the West when it came under the energetic direction of Persia, brought with it a general sense of insecurity and terror most favorable to religious excitement. Simultaneously with this the growth of democracy in the Greek city-states gave a new prominence to the popular faiths whose nature has just been analyzed, imposing them even on the higher classes and endangering the old aristocratic ideal of Sophrosyne, that is, self-limitation and self-control.

The Ionians had always been a colonizing race, and under the stress of Persian conquest their migratory tendency received an additional impulse. New settlements were founded in Southern Italy, and some of these became the homes of philosophic schools marked by extraordinary originality of thought, but somewhat lacking in the sanity and balance so characteristic of Ionian speculation in its first beginnings, steadied as these were by the traditions of an immemorial civilization.

The Pythagorean School. Considerable uncertainty prevails with regard to the chronology of the Italian Schools, and our authorities hold conflicting views about their origin and mutual relations. Pythagoras, whom for convenience we may take first, is an especially problematic figure. There is good contemporary evidence for the fact of his existence; but in what we are told about him the historical element (if any) is not easily distinguishable from the mythical. To be made the subject of marvelous legends- or inventions- is usually the fate of prophets or religious teachers rather than of philosophers; and in fact there is good reason to believe that Pythagoras belonged to both orders, to the lovers of simple knowledge- for whom, as will be remembered, he is said to have invented that incomparable name philosopher- and to those others who also claim truth for their heritage, but with a higher warrant than mere reason can give, to the class whom we generally call mystics.

According to the best of our information the life of Pythagoras extended through the greater part of the sixth century B.C., and ended with its close. Thus he came under the double influence of the scientific movement started by Thales, and of the great religious movement known as Orphicism. Orpheus was a mythical personage who stood godfather to a vast, spurious literature, the scriptures of a new Salvationist method, the worship of a dying god, and the hope of a blessed hereafter. Pythagoras associated this belief in immortality with the old Oriental doctrine of metempsychosis. He or his disciples taught that the eternal soul passed through a series of reincarnations, rising or falling in the scale of existence according as each earthly life had or had not been spent in accordance with the law of purity. As a help towards leading the perfect life Pythagoras founded a religious order to which women were admitted equally with men. At what period the sage began his social experiments is not known. Perhaps an attempt to set up the order in his native island of Samos may have excited the wrath of Polycrates, its brilliant and successful tyrant. At any rate, Pythagoras fled from Samos and settled in Croton, an Achaean colony on the Gulf of Tarentum. There, under his direction, the order flourished for many years until, like some more modern churches, it tried to obtain political supremacy in alliance with the aristocratic faction. A popular tumult, in which according to some accounts Pythagoras himself perished, put an end to the reforming movement is an organized community. But as a ferment of thought the school lived on, exercising an unparalleled influence on the whole later course of Greek philosophy, down to the final extinction of paganism under the Roman Empire.

Pythagorean Science and Philosophy. "Much learning does not give intelligence, or Pythagoras would have possessed it." So, with his usual scornfulness, wrote a somewhat later sage, the celebrated Heracleitus. And as a general principle the sarcasm is not without truth, as many a modern instance teaches. But it was not true of Pythagoras. If tradition may be trusted he had not only mastered all the knowledge of his age but had enriched it with important discoveries. He is said to have demonstrated the most fruitful proposition of elementary geometry, the theorem that the square on the base of a right-angled triangle equals the sum of the squares on the two containing sides. And he is also credited with the discovery that the height of notes on the musical scale is determined by the proportionate lengths of the chords by whose vibration they are produced, so that a vibrating string of half the length produces a note an octave higher. How much of the astronomy peculiar to his school goes back to its first founder we cannot tell. But he seems to have started that daring course of speculation which resulted between two and three centuries after his time in the theory, revived by Copernicus from Greek science, that the earth revolves on her own axis and is carried with the planets round the sun as the central orb of the system to which we belong. No European teacher has ever been so completely identified with his school as Pythagoras; and if this fact precludes any accurate distinction between the original contributions of the master to science and the subsequent additions made by his disciples, it makes the task of determining what was individual to him in philosophy almost impossible. In after ages the central Pythagorean doctrine undoubtedly was that all things are made out of number. Not, be it observed, that numbers or, more generally, mathematical relations constitute the very soul of nature, but that number is, like the Water of Thales or the Air of Anaximenes, the very stuff of which the world is made. But this seems too abstract a theory, not to say too subtle and elaborate, for so primitive a philosopher as Pythagoras himself to have constructed, even in outline; nor do we find any reference to it among his immediate successors.

What we do find them referring to as a current notion is the system of opposites, the idea that the universe is built up out of antithetical couples: the Limit and the Unlimited; the One and the Many; Rest and Motion; Light and Darkness; Good and Evil. To conceive things in general, and more particularly human affairs, under the form of balanced opposition was a fixed mental habit with the Greeks : our very word antithesis, taken straight from their language, still perpetuates that form of thought among ourselves; although no modern- not even Macaulay- has pushed its use to such excess. By its help Homer and Herodotus arrange their materials; by its laws the great sculptors disposed the reliefs on the pediments of the temples they had to adorn with groups of statuary; as a rhetorical artifice it disfigures the noble eloquence of Thucydides. In philosophy we find the employment of antithetical couples first exemplified by Anaximander, who, as will be remembered, assumes an eternal Infinite out of which the finite and perishable things of experience are formed, developing such contrasted qualities as heat and cold, dryness and wetness, by a process of differentiation from its homogeneous substance. We may suppose that the individual service of Pythagoras was to take up and generalize this fundamental idea, bringing the great social conflict of good and evil into line with the universal processes by which order is evolved out of chaos.

Heracleitus. So far the philosophers with whom we have had to deal have been little more than names, distinguished from one another by purely intellectual attributes, not recognizable as living personalities. But Greece was the very land of strongly-marked, vivid, individual characteristics, as the Homeric poems already show, and the personal note, so conspicuous for two centuries in her lyric poets, could not fail ultimately to make itself felt in the creations of abstract thought. It meets us for the first time in Heracleitus of Ephesus, universally acknowledged as the greatest of the pre-Socratic philosophers, and probably destined to rank for original genius among the greatest that the world has ever seen. We may add that with him the separation of philosophy from science in the strict sense begins. His interest lies solely with the one universal law of nature, possibly generalized from particulars, but not dependent on them, rather dictating to them what they shall be. Science and common sense have always protested against such an assumption: our own Francis Bacon has given the weightiest and most splendid expression to their protest; but others were found to utter it long before him. We have to ask, however, whether science itself could have dispensed with those paradoxes of pure thought, whether Bacon himself did not miss more truth by a servile adhesion to supposed facts than the Greeks missed by a sovereign disregard for them.

Our personal knowledge of Heracleitus comes almost entirely from what fragments of his composition survive; for no reliance can be placed on the stories current about his life, beyond the bare statement, confirmed by some references of his own, that he flourished at the end of the sixth century B.C. Thus, in the order of succession he comes immediately after Anaximenes, the last representative of the Milesian School; and in fact he seems to have followed the Milesian method of seeking for a universal principle, a substance of which all things are made. Two elements had already figured in that capacity. Water and Air. Heracleitus supersedes them by a third, which is Fire. He appeals to its function as a universal medium of exchange. "As goods are given for gold and gold for goods, so everything is given for fire and fire for everything." Our philosopher would have entered heartily into the modern speculation that every form of energy is electric and the whole material world merely so much congealed electricity.

For Heracleitus fire is what we now call the Absolute, the eternally self-existent reality underlying all appearance. "This order of things, the same for all, was not made by any god or any man, but was and is and will be for ever, a living fire, kindled by measure and quenched by measure." If any one likes to call the eternal One by the consecrated name of Zeus he may, only on the understanding, as seems to be hinted, that it is not to be the Zeus of the poets, "a magnified non-natural man," but an impersonal power, and a relation rather than a substance. There is an obvious contradiction in describing fire as both ever-living and as alternately kindled and quenched. And the Ephesian sage would not have hesitated for a moment to acknowledge that there was a contradiction. For, according to him, contradiction is the central fact of existence, the spring, as we should say now, that makes the wheels of the universe go round. In human affairs this is clear enough. "War is the father and king of all things": it originates our social distinctions, "making some gods and others men, some slaves and others free." Homer was wrong in wishing strife to perish; and he ought to be flogged out of the competitive games. It seems likely that the contempt of Heracleitus for Pythagoras may be explained by the same cause that accounts for his deprecatory estimate of Homer. When the Samian philosopher divided the great principles of nature into a series of antithetical couples he was right; but his whole system was vitiated by the failure to perceive that these opposites are necessary to each other's existence, that the whole frame of things is determined by their conflict and interplay. And that is just what makes fire so representative an element, so fit a type of the world-pervading law. Fire lives by struggling with and assimilating its own opposites, perishing at the moment of its complete triumph. Speaking more accurately, it only seems to perish, living again as air, whose birth is the death of fire, as similarly water lives by the death of air, earth by the death of water, and fire once more by the death of earth.

The Flux. This endless process of transformation was summed up by the Greeks in two words, not known to have been used by Heracleitus himself, but admirably expressing his philosophy: "all things flow". In some instances the universal flux is attested by the evidence of our senses; no man bathes twice in the same river; in others we know it by reason; "a new sun rises every day"- a conclusion deduced, we must suppose, from the fact that our own fires need perpetual supplies of fresh fuel to keep them burning. Solid earth must have proved, in more senses than one, a hard nut for the theory to crack; for thousands of years had still to pass before science could show that the most quiescent bodies are composed of molecules in a state of perpetual rotation and revolution. Probably Heracleitus argued that as earth is potentially fire, water, and air, it must partake in some way not evident to our imperfect senses of their mobility and evasiveness.

That which in material bodies presents the appearance of a perpetual flowing from one form to another, assumes in our sensations, appetites, and ideas the still higher aspect of a universal relativity. "If all things were turned to smoke the nostrils would distinguish them"; and in fact "souls do smell in the underworld";- where, as seems to be implied, everything is smoke. Fishes find salt water life-sustaining which to men is poisonous. "Asses prefer chopped straw to gold." "Swine bathe in mud, fowls in dust or ashes." "The most beautiful ape is ugly when compared with a man; the wisest or most beautiful man would be an ape compared with the gods." Good and evil are one. Physicians expect to be paid for inflicting all sorts of torments on their patients. "We should not know there was such a thing as justice did injustice not exist." "To God" or, as we should say, from the absolute point of view- "all things are fair and good and just. The distinction between just and unjust is human." "God is day and night, winter and summer, war and peace, plenty and famine." Yet for us also the union of opposites holds good. "Health, goodness, satiety, and rest are made pleasant by sickness, evil, hunger, and fatigue."

The Logos. Heracleitus might have pushed his negation of all the usual distinctions embalmed in common sense to a system of dissolving skepticism, in which every fixed principle, whether of knowledge or of action, would have disappeared. But he did not go to that extreme. After the doctrine of fire as the world element, after the dogma of an all-pervading relativity, comes the third and greatest idea of his philosophy, the idea of universal law and order. We have already come across it in that great sentence describing the Cosmos as an ever- living fire kindled and quenched "according to measure." The meaning is that fire transforms itself into water, water into earth, and so on on a basis of strict quantitative equivalence, so much of the one being paid in and so much of the other paid out. To the same effect we are told elsewhere that "the sun will not transgress his measures, or the Erinyes who guard Justice will find him out." In Greek mythology the Erinyes had for their original function to avenge the violated sanctities of blood- relationship, and more particularly to punish

28

the crime of matricide, a function subsequently extended to the punishment of all crime. By a crowning generalization they are here thought of as the guardians of natural law in the widest sense. Our philosopher calls this world-wide law by a name which had a great future before it. It is no other than the Logos, so familiar to us as the Word, proclaimed in the proem to St. John's Gospel, which became incarnate in Jesus Christ. St. John had derived it perhaps from Philo of Alexandria, Philo from the Stoics, and the Stoics from Heracleitus. To the Ephesian sage also, as to the fourth Evangelist, the Logos is the light that lighteth every man that cometh into the world the reason within him by which the cosmic Reason is revealed, his individual portion of the universal fire. For just as Anaximenes had assimilated the breath of life, the animating and sustaining spirit of man, with the all-constituting Air, Heracleitus assigns the same twofold activity to his elemental Fire. It was a common principle in Greek philosophy that like knows like; and so the burning stream of consciousness within us recognizes the eternal flux without- recognizes it also as reasonable, or rather as more reasonable in proportion to its vastly greater dominion and duration.

Agreement, community, identity are the essential notes of reality and reason. It will be remembered that the eternal order was, in modern phraseology, established as objectively true by being the same for all men. "All human laws draw their sustenance from the one divine law"; and to judge things truly we should hold fast to the common reason, even more forcibly than good citizens cling to the law of the State, which they defend like the city-wall, putting down the insolent self-assertion and arrogance of individuals. Individual sovereignty and the right of private judgment divorced from reason are fantastic illusions. Such individuality is at its height when we are asleep and dreaming, each of us in a world of his own. When we are awake it is the same world for all.

Not that Heracleitus believes in the wisdom of the

majority as an infallible guide. "Most people are foolish and bad; the good are few, and one man is worth ten thousand if he be the best." Nevertheless personal authority should go for nothing; arguments not words are the thing. Unfortunately argument is thrown away on the generality; as we saw, asses prefer chopped straw to gold. And the law of relativity itself explains why the law is not understood. Fire is only intelligible to the soul of fire, to the dry soul.

Degenerating minds in which the vital spark turns to water are thrown out of touch with the essence of things: theirs is a savor of death unto death. More particularly our prophet's own countrymen, the Ephesians, are a hopelessly irreformable set with a vicious hatred for superior persons as such. Better if the adult population were all to hang themselves and leave the city to their children. Such utterances are marked with the essentially aristocratic stamp of early Greek thought. It is probable that in the case of Heracleitus this contemptuous estimate of the vulgar was accentuated by a rationalistic disdain for the new popular religion. When he observes that the ritual of Dionysus would be shameless indecency were it not an act of divine worship, his reference, standing alone, might be meant for no more than an illustration of the universal relativity. But when taken in company with his attack on the Bacchic mysteries and the prevalent rage for secret ceremonies of all kinds, the words can only be interpreted as an unequivocal condemnation of the Orphic revival. Plato spoke no otherwise of the same manifestations a hundred and twenty years later, and Huxley's comments on Salvationism are less severe.

Xenophanes. Among those whom Heracleitus mentions as examples of learning without intelligence Xenophanes is one. In the order of time this philosopher, an Ionian of Colophon, precedes the great Ephesian ; but for our purposes he may be most conveniently studied in connection with a school developed in express opposition to the theory of a perpetual flux. I have called Xenophanes a philosopher; but he was primarily rather a poet of

alert and many-sided interests who spent a long life wandering
about Hellas and making a profession of reciting his own
compositions at the banquets of the rich. It would appear that the
conversation at such social gatherings largely consisted in
repeating fabulous stories about the quarrels of Titans and
Centaurs; and we know from Homer that scandalous ballads about
the amours of gods and goddesses were sometimes part of the
entertainment.

Xenophanes wished to introduce a higher tone, and as a
preliminary he attacks the mythology of the old poets with
uncompromising vigor. "Homer and Hesiod" he exclaims, "have
attributed to the gods everything that is a shame and reproach
among men- theft, adultery, and mutual deception." But not to
think of the gods as like bad men is merely the first step in true
religion; we should not think of them as like men at all. "Mortals
think that the gods are generated, that they have senses, a voice,
and a body like their own. The Ethiopians fancy that their deities
are black-skinned and snub-nosed; the Thracians give theirs fair
hair and blue eyes. If oxen or lions had hands and could paint they
too would make gods in their own image."

So much for the aristocratic, Olympian religion of the
poets. As to the popular Chthonian religion of the mysteries, with
its suffering and dying gods, he is reported to have dismissed it
with even briefer and more cutting sarcasm. Asked by the Eleates
should they sacrifice to Leucothea and mourn for her or not, he
advised them not to mourn if they believed her to be a goddess,
not to sacrifice if they believed her to be a woman. For himself
Xenophanes, like Anaximander, believed in an infinite source of
existence; but, unlike his Milesian predecessor, he identified this
one and eternal element with the visible earth, which he supposed
to stretch downward beneath our feet without end. This infinite
and eternal reality is God and the only God, resembling mortals
neither in form nor thought, but perceiving and thinking through
its whole extent.

EARLY GREEK PHILOSOPHY

We are told that Xenophanes created paleontology, pointing to the impressions of marine animals and plants found embedded in the quarries of Syracuse as evidence that what is now dry land was once water, teaching also that it would at some future period be covered with water once more- a theory probably suggested by Anaximander's idea that man was evolved from a fish-like creature.

Parmenides. Interesting in himself, Xenophanes interests us still more as the immediate predecessor of Parmenides, the poet-thinker to whom Elea, an otherwise obscure Ionian colony in Southern Italy, owes its immortal renown. Grown to manhood, as would seem, early in the fifth century B.C., and therefore a contemporary of the great Persian war, Parmenides comes a little later than Heracleitus, as whose polar opposite and complement he appears in the history of Greek philosophy. In point of genius there can be no comparison between them, Heracleitus was so much the greater of the two; indeed it is only within the last century that we have been able to appreciate his astonishing genius at something like its true value. At the same time, Parmenides had a more typically Greek mind, and therefore he counts for more in the history of Greek thought; indeed from Plato on his ideas dominate its evolution to the end.

It will be remembered that Pythagoras (or his followers) conceived reality under the form of so many antithetical couples, confronting each other in unreconciled opposition; the Limit and the Unlimited, the One and the Many, Rest and Motion, Light and Darkness, being the most conspicuous among them. And it will also be remembered that Heracleitus, while fully admitting the existence of such a pervading antithesis, refused to admit it as absolute. According to his interpretation, the members of each couple are necessary to each other's existence, are always passing into one another, are in truth at bottom the same thing. Now Parmenides, starting also from the Pythagorean conception, utterly rejects this theory, and even reacts so violently against it as to deny reality to what may be called the negative side of the antithesis. There are no such things as infinity, plurality, change, or darkness. The whole of being is one uniform, unchangeable, limited, luminous sphere, without parts, without a beginning, and without an end. He describes it in verses of great power and dignity, which may be translated as follows:

> "The Whole extends continuously,
> Being by Being set, immovable,
> Subject to the restraint of mighty bonds,
> Both increate and indestructible,
> Since birth and death have wandered far away,
> By true conviction into exile driven.
> The same in self-same place and by itself
> Abiding doth abide most firmly fixed,
> And bounded round by strong Necessity.
> Wherefore a holy law forbids that Being
> Should be without a bound, else want were there,
> And want of that would be a want of all."

To us moderns, with our habitual prostration before the idea of infinity, this dogmatic conclusion seems anything but self-evident; and "to be without a bound" strikes one as a proof of affluence rather than of destitution; but Parmenides here shows himself a true Greek, for to the Hellenic genius a boundary was associated with finish rather than with finitude.

The Theory of Being. It has been suggested that the Parmenidean conception of Being as something without movement, variety, or change is not meant to describe the world of sense and experience, but rather the hidden reality that underlies sensible appearances, the world as revealed to pure intelligence, the thing in itself of modern metaphysics. This, however, is an entire misconception. Early Greek thought had not risen to the idea of a fundamental distinction between reality and appearance; the delusions it recognized were occasional, accidental, individual errors of perception, not inherent in human perception as such. What is more, Parmenides leaves no sort of doubt as to his meaning. He tells us that only what is can be conceived or even spoken of; the non-existent is also the unthinkable. Moreover, what is can never not have been, can never cease to be. In other words, what most philosophers still believe of the world as a whole, what most men of science till lately believed of material atoms or of the smallest pulses of energy- that they are "both increate and indestructible"- this Parmenides believed so absolutely and universally that for him the conviction excluded the possibility even of movement and change. Suppose a body passes from one place to another, or suppose its color to be altered, say, from green to red- in either case something that was has ceased to be, something is now that was not before. And so the very first law of existence would be broken, being would be identical with non-being, in fact just what was taught by Heracleitus, whose very words are quoted in this connection as a vain thing.

There is another and even stronger reason for interpreting the absolute reality of Eleatic philosophy as no mysterious ideal existence, but a direct object of sensuous perception. Parmenides describes it as not only bounded, but as shaped like a perfect sphere, extending equally in all directions from a central point. And his words so evidently apply to the visible world that all subsequent thinkers who came under his influence continued for many centuries to regard the material universe as a perfect sphere.

This conception had its root in a great scientific discovery- no less a discovery than that the earth is a globe. Before Parmenides no Greek was aware of the fact, nor perhaps was any Oriental astronomer. Thales and his successors were, in more senses than one, quite at sea on the subject. Xenophanes, with every opportunity, through a long life, of assimilating the most advanced ideas of his age, thought that the earth stretched-downwards to infinity. Now, whether Parmenides himself actually discovered the earth's sphericity is not quite certain. We can only say that there is good authority for believing that he did. That he knew it to be a fact is therefore highly probable. And this fact, so astounding, so contrary to common opinion, would influence his whole way of thinking. Its suggestiveness would, so to speak, go to his head. A sphere is the one absolutely perfect thing in experience, excluding change, excluding variety, without beginning or end, the very type of what is finished. And now it turns out that earth, the greatest thing we know, is a sphere. No more remained than to represent all existence on the same model and to invest it with every imaginable perfection.

Astronomy was not the only positive science that influenced the thought of Parmenides. As a South Italian Greek he must have come into touch with the Pythagoreans; indeed we have seen reason to believe that his severe monism was a protest against their dualistic view of nature. And apart from such ultimate questions he would have much to learn from them about geometry, in which they were at that time the world's acknowledged masters. Now geometry is the science of space; and it will be found on examination that Parmenides in enumerating the properties of Being almost identifies them with the properties of absolute space. It is extended, continuous, homogeneous, unchanging, with parts completely immovable among one another. He did not indeed conceive it as infinite; but for the Greek philosophers, as for modern mathematicians, the infinity of space remained an open question. What really differentiated his view from ours was the ascription of intelligence to that rigid unalterable sphere. We habitually think of mind as the inextended; to Parmenides mind and extension were one and the same. And we need only place ourselves at his point of view to see why this should be. From the beginning Greek thought had retained much of that animism which is the sole philosophy of primitive men.

Not to repeat what has already been pointed out in the case of the Milesian School, Xenophanes in identifying the world with God had described it as perceiving and thinking through its whole infinite extent. And Heracleitus had represented the reasonable principle within ourselves as a fiery particle, able by virtue of its common nature to recognize and act in harmony with the cosmic fire by which the universe is shaped and directed. Parmenides moves on the same lines with his predecessors, but goes a step beyond them. According to him mind and its object are not merely akin; they are the same. Nor indeed was any other conclusion compatible with the first principle of his system, that difference neither does nor can exist. Or again, we may say that the world without has been simplified down to pure extension; the world within has been simplified down to pure reason, which, as it merely repeats and reflects that external uniformity, is logically indistinguishable from it.

After his uncompromising enunciation of absolute truth, Parmenides made the concession to common opinion of writing a sequel to his First Philosophy on the lines of old Ionian speculation, in which a place is given to those negative elements of darkness, cold, and opacity which he had begun by dismissing as unthinkable. A theory of evolution found its place here, leading up to what would now be called a materialistic view of mind, as determined by the excess of some one element in the composition of man's bodily organization. But these were accommodations to the world's opinions that the world has willingly let die. It was by his relentless paradoxes, not by his contemptuous concessions, that Parmenides exercised a decisive influence on the subsequent courses of thought. And it was through their combination with the almost equally daring paradoxes of Heracleitus that the element of truth contained in the respective systems of these two great men told for all that it was worth.

CHAPTER III

THE ANALYTICAL PHILOSOPHERS

Zeno of Elea. Parmenides seems never to have made more than one disciple. This was a young Eleate named Zeno, to whom he was united not only by common opinions but by the bonds of devoted private affection. Yet closely as they agree in principle, the two thinkers belong to distinct ages with widely contrasted tendencies and methods; the one dogmatic, the other argumentative; the one more comprehensive, the other more analytic; the one potent to unite and simplify; the other excelling in subtlety and minuteness.

What struck people most about the philosophy of Parmenides was that it denied motion; and to such a laughter-loving race as the Greeks this paradox gave much occasion for ridicule. Zeno came to his master's assistance by showing, or attempting to show, that the idea of motion involves greater difficulties than its denial; and this he did by a series of examples whose interest is not exhausted even for the speculation of our own times. His most celebrated puzzle is that known as Achilles and the tortoise. Let us suppose that there is a race between the two, and that the tortoise is allowed a start, say, of ten feet; then Achilles will never overtake his slow-footed competitor, for while he is getting over the first ten feet the tortoise will have accomplished, say, one foot, or as much less than that as you please. Anyhow it will be some measurable distance, however small. Then while Achilles is traversing that space the tortoise will have advanced through the same fraction of it as before, and so on ad infinitum. It is no answer to say that as a matter of fact the swifter does always overtake the slower runner; the question is how space can be conceived except as infinitely divisible, and how, granting that, an infinite number of divisions can be run through in a finite time.

It has been suggested as a solution that the infinite divisibility of time makes this possible. But, in fact, it only doubles the difficulty, for then we have two infinite series to be run out instead of one.

Skeptical arguments are dangerous allies to dogmatic theories; and Zeno's method might have been turned with destructive effect against his master. For it goes to disprove the possibility of continuously extended space as a thing in itself; and this Parmenides had assumed without question; nor indeed was it questioned until thousands of years after his time.

Empedocles. Change and motion held their own notwithstanding all that the Eleatics could say to prove their impossibility. But Parmenides by his daring paradoxes had brought into full view an aspect of the truth that Heracleitus, going to the opposite extreme, had tended to obscure, and that common sense had yet to learn as something self-evident when it was once stated. This was the perpetuity through all change of a reality underlying appearance, a substance that is neither created nor destroyed. We may say that the Ionians had practically assumed the existence of such a substance, variously identifying it with one of the so-called elements- water, air, earth, or fire. But their analysis had been what chemists call qualitative rather than quantitative. They did not sharply formulate the generalization that matter persists through all metamorphoses without loss or gain. Heracleitus alone, with his wonderful sagacity, grazed but did not grasp this law. Fully to realize it was reserved for the inferior genius of Empedocles.

Empedocles stands as an isolated, somewhat problematic, figure among the early Greek philosophers. By exception he was not an Ionian but a Dorian; by exception not an aristocrat but a democrat. His restless and insatiable vanity also makes an unpleasant contrast with the singular personal majesty of the rest. For the first though not for the last time in history, he makes us feel that to be a charlatan and a great thinker are not incompatible predicates.

His birthplace may have had something to do with his ambiguous character and attitude. This was Acragas, the modern Girgenti, a Sicilian city, renowned for the luxury of its inhabitants and the splendor of its public edifices, still as ruins pre-eminent among the glories of Doric architecture. It was a chief seat of the Chthonian religion, whose two great goddesses, Demeter and Persephone, were especial objects of popular worship. Standing, moreover, almost on the frontier between Hellenic and Phoenician civilization, Acragas was exposed in a peculiar way to the evil influences of Semitic example with the least restraint from the old Greek traditions of Sophrosyne, of self-knowledge and self-control. Empedocles tells his countrymen that he walked through the Sicilian cities crowned with garlands, honored as an immortal god, followed by crowds of men and women entreating him to heal their diseases, to give them oracles, to show them the way to gain.

What the multitude asked from Empedocles was no more than his philosophy undertook to give. His disciples were to learn the arts by which old age is warded off, the winds controlled, and the dead restored to life. Our prophet claimed, in fact, to be nothing less than a fallen divinity, who in some far distant pre-natal stage of existence had stained himself with bloodshed, and was condemned as an expiation of his guilt to pass through a long cycle of existences, vegetable, animal, and human, as a dweller in the water, in the air, or on the earth. Apparently the period of purification was now nearly complete, and his restoration to the abodes of the blessed in sight. Like the sages of the Far East he preaches the kinship of all living things, the sacredness of animal life, and the pollution incurred by eating meat. A deep vein of Oriental pessimism also enters into his theory of existence.

Standing alone such utterances might be interpreted as no

more than an enthusiastic expression of the new Orphic religion, derived proximately from the Pythagorean schools of South Italy. The puzzling thing is that they have come down to us in close association with a thoroughly materialistic philosophy, where no place seems to be left for an immortal human soul, and hardly even for gods, except as poetic names for the elements and forces of nature. Empedocles lived towards the middle of the fifth century B.C. One is tempted to think of him as a "modernist" in reference to the religion of his age, giving a mythological coloring to speculations really destructive of all mythology.

The Four Elements. "No wise man," the Sicilian philosopher tells us, "would imagine that (mortals) had no existence before their birth, and will have none after their dissolution." These words might be taken to imply the soul's eternity. But probably they mean no more than that the body is composed of imperishable parts. Empedocles is credibly reported to have been a pupil of Parmenides; and he repeats the master's assertion that what is can neither begin nor cease to be, but without pushing it to the extent of denying all reality to change and motion. What men call birth and death are simply a mixture and separation of pre-existing substances. Fire, air, earth, and water are the ultimate elements whence all things arise and into which they return. Each of these had been erected by one or other of the Ionian thinkers into the sole principle of nature: Empedocles follows the facile method of eclectics in every age by granting equal rights to all.

And his philosophy has left a permanent stamp on language which the discoveries of modern chemistry have not been able to efface.

Love and Strife. The tendency to harmonize and combine carries him on to a further and more daring speculative effort. Parmenides has to be reconciled not only with common sense but also with Heracleitus. Experience tells us that the world is not now

constituted as a perfect homogeneous sphere in the way dreamed
of at Elea; but that happy consummation has been reached already
in the eternal revolutions of existence, and will be reached again.
Two powers control the universal process, Love and Strife; Love
drawing the elements into one. Strife tearing them apart; and the
whole world cycle passes through four phases distinguished by
their alternating predominance and decline. As Love gains ground
things draw together; when it triumphs they are united in the
perfect sphere, but only to fly asunder on their way to complete
separation when Strife becomes lord of the ascendant. We are now
on the down-grade; that is to say, we are living in a period of
increasing differentiation and ever greater subjection of nature to
the law of Strife. Empedocles may have been led to this gloomy
diagnosis by the sentence in which Heracleitus speaks of war as
the father of all things.

Love and Strife answer in some ways to the attractive and
repulsive forces of modern science. But they are conceived as
material or at least as extended objects, with just as much, or as
little, self-consciousness as the four elements. We ourselves are
composed of all six; and as like is only known by like, we
recognize the presence of each in the external world through that
portion of it which helps to make up our separate individuality.

Theory of Sensation. A current phrase speaks of the
external world as known to us through the channels of sense. The
phrase is now merely metaphorical, but it contains a reminiscence
of what Empedocles thought literal truth. He imagined that
streams of material particles emanated from the bodies about us,
and that these made their way through certain minute passages or
pores with which the organs of sense are supplied, thus producing
the characteristic sensation by which the element within is enabled
to recognize the element from without as akin to itself There is an
exact adaptation between the particles and the pores of the same
element, so that fire, for example, is only penetrable by fire, and
water by water. By this theory, much more than by his ambitious

cosmology, Empedocles showed himself an original and progressive thinker, in harmony, like Zeno, with the minutely analytical tendencies of his age, and contributing far more than Zeno to the subsequent development of speculation.

Glimpses of Modern Science. Like his Ionian predecessors the wonder-working Acragantine poet has a place in the history of science no less than in the history of philosophy. He divined the truth that light travels with an appreciable velocity; he knew that the revolution of one body round another can only be maintained by the composition of two forces, a centrifugal and a centripetal; and he recognized the sexual reproduction of plants. He even suggested the famous doctrine of the non-survival of the unfit, afterwards borrowed from him by Lucretius. And if we could take the account already referred to of his triumphal progress through Sicily as less an expression of intoxicated personal vanity than a dream of the victories in store for human knowledge, no Greek would be so justly entitled to the name of a prophet.

Melissus. Empedocles founded no school. After him the scene changes once more to East Hellas, and the language of philosophy relapses from poetry to sober prose. But through all external vicissitudes the new method of infinitesimal analysis is maintained, leading to fresh conquests in the invisible world. Change of scene was indeed the best possible security for continued progress. It saved speculation from sinking into a routine. Unlike Moab, the Greek genius did not "settle on its lees," but was "emptied from vessel to vessel," escaping the reproach of a taste that remains and a scent that is not changed.

In East Hellas, as in Sicily, the problem was to reconcile Heracleitus with Parmenides, the theory of an unceasing flux with the theory of an unchanging reality. We may assume that the Ephesian philosophy was well known and widely canvassed in those parts ever since its first introduction, seeing that its fame had spread within a few years to Italy. And we have proof positive that the Eleatic philosophy was studied in Ionia by a contemporary of Empedocles, the Samian admiral Melissus, who defeated an Athenian fleet in the year 440 B.C. This remarkable man, the only speculative sailor mentioned in all history, wrote a prose treatise, of which considerable fragments survive, reproducing the main ideas of Parmenides with some important variations. Unlike the master, he declared that the eternal reality was without a bound-identifying it, as would seem, with infinite space; and while denying movement or multiplicity to absolute Being, he allows them at least a place in thought as illusions of sense. Such an enlargement of view meant much, how much will be apparent when we come to study the grandest result of early Greek thought, the Atomic Theory.

Atomism. Before explaining how the theory of atoms arose, let me explain what it means. Atomism implies first of all that matter, or the substance of which bodies are composed, while it occupies space and is therefore extended, is not, like pure space, continuous, but discrete. That is, it consists of perfectly distinct and separate parts, moving about in void space, solid, indivisible, impenetrable, differing from one another only in size and shape, capable of being united together in mechanical groups, but only communicating with one another by external contact and collision. In the next place, the atoms are so small as to lie beyond the reach of our senses; but, assuming space to be infinitely extended, they are infinite in number, for otherwise the universe would in the course of infinite ages have disappeared by dissipation into the surrounding void. They are also eternal; for the least tendency to decay acting through endless time would equally have involved their total annihilation before the present date. And, being indestructible, there is no reason to suppose that they ever began to exist, not to mention the general inconceivability that out of nothing something could arise.

Evidently the atom of Greek philosophy is an

incomparably more meager idea than the atom of modern science with its formidable outfit of energies, conceived as endowed with gravitation, cohesion, elasticity, radio-activity, electro-magnetic properties, and chemical affinities. At the same time we must remember that all this elaborate mechanism has been built up stone by stone on the simple foundation supplied by the constructive genius of two Ionian Greeks, Leucippus, whose birthplace is unknown, and Democritus, a native of Abdera on the barbarous Thracian coast, enjoying little popularity in their lifetime and unhonoured after death even by the inheritors who traded most successfully on their discoveries.

Leucippus. From the scanty information supplied to us on the subject it appears that Leucippus, the real founder of atomism, lived a little after Empedocles and Melissus. Generalizing from the doctrine of subtle material emanations as the cause of external perception, put forward by the one, he would form the conception of multitudinous invisible particles as the basis of all real existence. And the infinite space of the other, dissociated from its material contents, would supply him with the equally essential conception of a void giving full scope for their movement and interplay. By a remarkable anticipation of what is now called atomicity he supposed that these particles or at least some of them were supplied with little hooks by which they became woven into chains and membranes, ultimately forming, so to speak, the cell-wall of a closed universe, within which the cosmic evolution of order out of chaos was conducted. "Nothing," he said, "happens by chance, everything by law and necessity"- or, as we should say, by purely mechanical causation.

For the original cause of motion Greek atomism refers us to weight, which at that time seemed to be an inseparable quality of matter. It had not yet been discovered that the fall of heavy bodies was connected with a tendency to move towards the center of the earth; nor was it known that bodies falling in a vacuum move with equal velocities, so that collisions between them cannot occur. Accordingly Leucippus credited all his atoms alike with a downward motion through infinite space; and he supposed that the larger atoms, having a greater velocity than the smaller, would overtake, collide, and become entangled with them. As the knowledge of astronomy and physics spread, the inconsistency of this primitive atomism with natural law came to be understood, and therefore no man of science after Democritus ever adopted it in antiquity, although the contrary has been stated by ill-informed literary critics in our own day.

Democritus. Democritus seems to have adopted the atomic theory of Leucippus without any essential modification. What distinguishes him as a philosopher is the enormous range of his interests. We have seen that the love of knowledge for its own sake was recognized at a very early time as the characteristic feature in philosophy. Democritus expressed this passion vividly by saying, "I had rather discover a single new explanation than be King of Persia." But his ambition went beyond a knowledge of things, which, taken alone, is merely science. He asked what was the nature of knowledge itself, thus giving a still wider extension to philosophy, of which that question has ever since formed an integral part. And he seems to have been the first to point out the distinction, since grown so familiar, between the two great sources of knowledge; sense which gives us the appearances, and understanding which gives us the reality, of things. He owed it to the atomic theory. Atomism is a reasonable inference from our sensations, but, at the same time, in a way, it denies them. As he puts it, "sweet and bitter, hot and cold, exist by convention"- or, as we now say, subjectively- "color exists by convention; in reality, atoms and the void." So little truth is there in the reproach commonly brought against the materialists, of whom Democritus was a precursor, that they believe nothing but the evidence of their senses.

Moral Philosophy. Philosophy, however, is not complete even when we have added a theory of knowing to our theory of being. Man is by nature not only contemplative but active, and even more active than contemplative. Accordingly if we would attain true universality, to those other theories a theory of practice must be added. And just as he who takes all knowledge for his province must needs simplify the task by an effort of extreme generalization, by going back to first principles, by singling out the fundamental element, or the original cause, or the widest law of things, or again by fixing on the true criterion of knowledge, so also the supreme master of practice will make it his object to pick out from the infinite details of social intercourse, politics, industry, and fine art, the absolute end to which everything else is a means, which alone gives a real value to all those multifarious activities. In a word, as the later Greeks put it, after physics and logic comes ethics or the philosophy of conduct.

It proves the wonderful genius of Democritus as a systematizing thinker that he took not only the second step but the third. Here also, as in the case of the Milesian school, with their general theories of the world as a natural growth, the absence of an organized priesthood teaching a fixed theology was essential to speculative freedom. After the first outburst of scientific speculation there had indeed been a danger that the great religious revival we call Orphicism might intervene to check its further progress, at least in the direction of bringing conduct also under natural law; and not to speak of the Pythagoreans, there are very marked symptoms in Empedocles of a desire to keep well with the mystical movement, a nervous anxiety to disclaim too great freedom of thought. Now, for the atomists at least there could be no such obscurantist leanings. While formally acknowledging the possible existence of superhuman beings, their theory left no place for gods in any true sense of the word; in a world where the atoms alone were eternal, where necessity and mechanical law alone ruled, there could be neither creation, nor providence, nor immortality.

Democritus in fact boldly explained theology as a

primitive personification of natural objects. At the time when Democritus taught, which seems to have been in the last third of the fifth century B.C., ethics was, as it still continues to be, much less advanced than physical science. But the facts of moral experience being better known left less room for error. Thus what he had to say on the subject took the form of proverbial philosophy, of short sentences, true so far as they go, but not worked up into systematic form. They are not inspired by the great social enthusiasm of Plato and the Stoics; but neither is there the low standard vulgarly supposed to go with philosophical materialism. The highest end is declared to be a contented mind, which is won by avoiding excess and by fixing the desires not on sensual indulgences but on imperishable things. Sins are to be avoided not from fear but from a sense of duty. Goodness is not abstinence from doing wrong, but from the wish to do wrong. Encouragement and persuasion are a better training to virtue than law and compulsion. The whole world is the fatherland of a good soul. Yet our aphorist is too genuine a Greek to merge political duty in a vague cosmopolitanism. He tells us to put the interests of the state above all others, not grasping at more power for ourselves than is good for the community. For a well-administered city best secures the safety of all. Democritus has been called "the laughing philosopher" because a late legend describes him as always making merry over the follies and vices of mankind. As it happens this silly story is sufficiently answered by one of his own maxims. "Men should not laugh but mourn over each other's misfortunes." And to those who know Heracleitus at first hand the parallel designation of him as "the weeping philosopher" must seem an equally infelicitous description of his lofty contempt for the common herd.

Anaxagoras. Anaxagoras of Clazomenae, who has been reserved for the last place in this chapter, was older than any of the thinkers who have so far been dealt with in it; but as a link with the schools of Athens it will be found more convenient to discuss his teaching after that of the atomists, with the earliest form of which he may have had some acquaintance. Our informants tell us that Anaxagoras was born about 500 B.C., that he settled in Athens when entering on middle age, and remained there for thirty years. His was the true philosophic temperament. Asked what made life worth living, he replied, "contemplating the heavens and the universal order." The great statesman Pericles was his pupil and friend. Euripides is mentioned among his admirers, and is believed to have had the Ionian sage in mind when he wrote these noble lines:

> "Happy is he who has learned
> To search out the secret of things,
> Not for the citizens' bane,
> Neither for aught that brings
> An unrighteous gain.
> Bat the ageless order he sees
> Of Nature that cannot die,
> And the causes whence it springs,
> And the how and the why.
> Never have thoughts like these
> To a deed of dishonor been turned."

(Translated by Madame Duclaux.)

In their religious beliefs, however, neither Pericles nor Euripides represented average public opinion at Athens. There may have been as superstitious communities in Hellas: none were so suspicious of new views or so intolerant. Possibly the wonderful cleverness of the Athenians made them more keenly alive than other Greeks to the dissolving effect of the new speculations on the old beliefs. We have seen that, in fact, from Thales on, the radical incompatibility between the two was becoming more and more obvious. A crisis was bound to come at last, and it came at a spot where political animosities and democratic jealousies helped to organize the forces of reactionary prejudice.

A Martyr of Science. In the year 432 an attempt was made to dislodge Pericles from the position he had long occupied as the trusted leader of the Athenian people. For tactical reasons his assailants began by bringing charges of impiety against Aspasia, his wife in all but the name, the great sculptor Pheidias, whom he had employed for the embellishment of the Acropolis, and Anaxagoras. The charges against Aspasia and Pheidias were of a frivolous character and do not concern us here. Against the Clazomenian philosopher there was, unhappily, a very strong case. He taught that the sun was a red-hot mass of stone, larger than the Peloponnesus, that the stars were not fire, that the moon was an earthy body, shining by reflected light, with an irregular surface, and partially built over. Now at Athens the sun and moon passed for being blessed gods, and a pious belief prevailed that they were worshiped as such by the whole human race. To treat them as lumps of inanimate matter seemed therefore not only irreligious but absurd.

According to some of our authorities Anaxagoras was tried for blasphemy and condemned. According to others he escaped condemnation by a timely flight from Athens. It seems certain that he ended his days at Lampsacus in an honored old age among a people who contrived to reconcile their reverence for the sun and moon with their reverence for intellectual and moral grandeur. At his own desire the philosopher's death was annually commemorated by giving a holiday to the children of the town. His image may still be seen on the coins of his native place, Clazomenae, probably copied from a statue erected there in his honor.

Qualitative Atomism. Democritus observed with truth that the astronomical heresies which brought Anaxagoras into such trouble were not new. Nor was it new to say- although a fragment of his states it as something paradoxical and unfamiliar- that what people commonly call becoming and perishing is really the combination and separation of pre-existent parts. For Empedocles had preceded him in starting with this assumption. The originality of Anaxagoras lay in giving this great principle an extension undreamed of by any of his predecessors or contemporaries. According to him, not only does the mass of matter remain a fixed quantity, but its qualities also are permanent, that is such properties as temperature, color, smell, and the like. There is always the same amount of these in the world, more or less latent, more or less apparent, as they are more or less confused or distinct. In the beginning the confusion was infinite; analysis might have gone on for ever without arriving at an ultimate element that did not combine all shapes, temperatures, colors, smells, and tastes. What the atomists declared to exist only "by convention," or in modern parlance "subjectively," is "objective," real, eternal. And even now the separation of qualities is not perfect. Everything contains a trace of everything else. What we say of human nature, that no man is quite without good or without evil, without wisdom or without folly, Anaxagoras said of all nature.

Nous. How then from the primal confusion did the present world of order, of at least relative distinction arise? The answer is strong and simple. "All things were together: then Nous (Reason) came and disposed them in order." Such words suggest the idea of an intelligent First Cause; and in fact that was what Greek readers at first took them to mean. But it has always remained doubtful what Anaxagoras himself understood by Nous. In some respects he clearly conceived it as like human reason, but with far greater powers. It "knows everything about everything and controls everything." On the other hand, if not exactly a material, it is an extended substance, "the thinnest and purest of all things,"- unmixed with the elements, and enabled by this absolute separateness, of which it is a unique example, to act on them. Its action, however, is of a merely mechanical kind, and has no other effect than to set up a vortical movement by which the component elements of the original mixture are segregated, what is unlike being parted and what is like being thrown together.

If, as seems the only possible interpretation of his words, Parmenides identified pure reason with pure space or extension, we may presume that Anaxagoras adopted this view from the Eleatic philosophy. Some modern thinkers have called space "the possibility of movement"; and paradoxical as the idea may seem to us, an ancient thinker may well have expressed the connection between the two by saying that space was the cause of motion. Such a confusion had, indeed, already become quite incredible to Plato and Aristotle. They supposed that when Anaxagoras talked about Reason as an ordering power he meant something like the reason of an architect or a legislator; and so when in the sequel they found him treating the evolution of the universe as a process of mechanical causation they could not reconcile such materialism in the details of the system with the spiritualism of its first principle. On the other hand, the modern interest in evolution as at first an unconscious process and only becoming self-reflective in its last stages, gives us perhaps a clearer insight into the true significance of Nous than was possible to the great founders of idealism. To describe it as an anticipation of Herbert Spencer would of course be an anachronism. Yet there is at least a germ of the "differentiation and integration" that Spencer made so much of in the activity ascribed to the cosmic Nous by Anaxagoras. And perhaps it was the consciousness of their own reason as a discriminating and identifying faculty that led both philosophers to look on all nature as exemplifying the same process on a far vaster scale.

Diogenes of Apollonia. As it happens, the Greek word of which differentiation is the exact equivalent was first brought into use by Diogenes of Apollonia, a second-rate Dorian eclectic who popularized the study of natural philosophy at Athens by combining the doctrine of Anaxagoras with that of Anaximenes. Anaximenes had taught that Air was the fundamental principle of existence, the substance out of which all things are made, the animating soul of man and the great conservative force of nature. Diogenes took the further step of identifying this elemental Air with the Nous, thus, as might seem, giving more prominence to the material and mechanical side of the latter. In point of fact, however, he laid more stress than Anaxagoras on the evidences of design in nature, the beautiful harmonies of which, according to him, could only be explained as the work of an intelligent cause. During the fifth century great progress was made by the Greeks in the study of physiology; and this science came to exercise an even more decisive influence on speculation than mathematics and astronomy. We see this in Diogenes, who was indeed a doctor by profession; and the idea of differentiation, to which, as has been said, he first gave a name, would be especially brought home to him by his knowledge of the human organism, affording as this does a most complete example of the division of labor. Of course the uses of its various parts were then very imperfectly understood; but Diogenes was sagacious enough to conjecture that the vascular system, of which he wrote a careful account, had something to do with the distribution of air- or, as we should say, oxygen- over the whole body; and he acutely explained the absence of intelligence in plants to their want of such a system.

Aristophanes. Aristophanes, the great comic dramatist of the age, wrote a play called The Clouds, satirizing the philosophers, in the year 423 B.C., and from this we can gather that the system of Diogenes was then the fashionable philosophy at Athens. The poet had no eye for the religious value of the new theories, regarding them solely as an impious attempt to substitute material agencies for the time-honored Olympian divinities, with the belief in whom he conceived the interests of private morality to be inseparably bound up. In this respect he thoroughly represented the public opinion of Athens, already exhibited in the persecution of Anaxagoras, and destined under the guidance of the greatest Athenian thinkers to lead Greek philosophy away from the physical studies it had pursued with such success into other directions more in harmony with the religious genius of the city where it was henceforth to find a home.

CHAPTER IV

THE SOPHISTS

Education at Athens. Speculative freedom, complete everywhere else in the Hellenic world, was, as we have seen, not complete at Athens. But in that city which called herself the school of Greece, education always remained free, to this extent at least, that it was a matter of individual enterprise. Although in other ways sufficiently absorbing and despotic, the State neither provided the means of instruction nor did it attempt to prescribe what the course of instruction should be. Apparently any one that liked could open a school, and fathers could send their sons to any school they liked. The system seems to have worked well. Every Athenian citizen could read to some extent, and it was considered rather disreputable not to read well. Boys of the higher classes were also taught to write, to play on the lyre, and to repeat a good deal of poetry by heart. In the best times of the republic they were also trained to be hardy, obedient, and pure In later life some people continued to read literature besides hearing some of the greatest things that were ever written, in the theater, and some of the greatest things that were ever spoken, in the public assemblies. Booksellers' shops existed, and there is reason to believe that even so abstruse a work as that of Anaxagoras could be bought for a drachma- a little under tenpence in our money. Educated women are mentioned as a class by Plato in the fourth century B.C., and we are told that tragedies were their favorite reading, as indeed of most persons, which, considering the austerity of the Greek tragic drama, shows a considerable refinement of taste.

What we call the higher or University education was a creation of philosophy, and had only just begun to dawn in the age of Pericles. At first young men entering on public life learned what it was essential for them to know about the world and about great affairs from some older friend to whom they were attached by ties of affectionate intimacy. Sometimes they profited also by conversing with women of genius. Under a free government the power of speech is the surest road to success. Hence in modern democracies lawyers command a disproportionate share of political influence. In old Athens there was no such profession: as prosecutor or as defendant every one had to plead his own cause before a large popular jury. Thus, even apart from any ambition to lead the State, every citizen was interested in mastering the arts both of cross-examination and of continuous delivery; while to men of high birth and wealth, being marked out as special objects of attack for political opponents and blackmailers, address in using the weapons of tongue-fence became even a matter of life and death. In course of time litigants made up to some extent for the want of counsel by employing a professional hand to write a speech for them which they then learned by heart and delivered in court as if it had been their own composition. This practice, however, although it might relieve the mass of Athenian citizens from the necessity of studying rhetoric as an art, left the demand for a professional training in rhetoric unaffected, as the speech-writers themselves required to be educated for their work.

Philosophy and Rhetoric. Philosophy as the study of things in themselves does not seem at first sight in any way related to rhetoric- at least not to the rhetoric of law-courts and deliberative assemblies where human interests are the subject of discussion, and appeals to human passion the means adopted by a skillful speaker for making his opinions prevail. It must, however, be borne in mind that Greek philosophy owed its origin to the schools of science, a circumstance which from the beginning brought it into connection with the practice of teaching; that it systematized the habit of taking wide views, so characteristic, even in Homer, of Greek eloquence; that the earliest sages had something to say about man as well as about nature, while their successors gave an ever greater place to the laws of life and conduct as the evolution of thought went on; and finally that a knowledge of the world's secrets, by raising its possessor above all petty cares, interests, and prejudices, surrounded him with a certain halo of intellectual and moral superiority well calculated to impose on a Greek audience. For these reasons the two seemingly independent spheres of rhetoric and philosophy- the study of words and the study of things- expanded until they met and overlapped, a wide range of subjects being either treated as common ground or hotly disputed between the rival teachers who regarded education from opposite points of view.

It was agreed that the youth of good family, after he had left school, needed some further training as a preparation for taking part in public or private business with credit to himself and his ancestry. In other words, there was a demand for the higher education. And just as now, it was a moot-point what, that education should consist of, above all what place, if any, should be held in it by religion and morality; morality more particularly occupying the very center of the ground shared or disputed between rhetoric and philosophy. Not that a contemporary of Aristophanes used such abstract terms as religion and morality to express his meaning ; but he had consecrated traditions of belief and conduct which may conveniently be summed up under those two names, and which meant for him all that religion and morality mean for us.

The Sophists. The demand for higher education called into existence a class of teachers known as Sophists. In modern language a sophist is one who uses fallacious arguments, knowing them to be such. When Aristotle wrote, the name bore a still more opprobrious significance, for he defines it as one who reasons falsely for the sake of gain. In earlier times, however, this was not so, for Pindar and Herodotus use sophist in an altogether creditable sense, as meaning a man of superior skill or wisdom, whether he happened to be a great philosopher or an ordinary intellectual craftsman. What seems to have first raised a prejudice against this originally honorable appellation was the emergence of certain persons who professed to teach wisdom and virtue in

Return for a substantial payment. Money-making as such was not thought disreputable in good Greek society, for even so haughtily aristocratic a poet as Pindar wrote odes to order. But then it must be remembered that a poem, like a picture or a statue, seems to possess a certain tangible reality making it a more appropriate equivalent for so much hard cash than such purely ideal values as wisdom and virtue, which also are universally associated with a considerable indifference to this world's goods. And this feeling would be still further strengthened by the fact that no philosopher had ever exacted a fee from his pupils. Again, for reasons already stated, that higher education which the sophists sold to rich young men always included a training in rhetoric. Now an Athenian who was used to hear rival statesmen supporting opposite policies in the Assembly and rival pleaders presenting mutually contradictory views of law and fact to the popular tribunals, must have had it strongly borne in on him that while one speaker was certainly wrong each in turn managed to make it seem that he was right- a clear proof that one of them at least knew the art of making the worse appear the better reason. From whom could they have learned this nefarious art but from their sophist teachers; and was it not scandalous that a class of persons should exist who made it their profession, and a very lucrative profession also, to pervert the moral principles of the community?

Again, as all philosophers were popularly called sophists, and as all attempted to explain meteorological phenomena by other than divine agencies, besides expressing more or less paradoxical opinions about the nature of things in general, the paid teachers of wisdom got the credit of what the vulgar considered the impieties and absurdities of philosophy. And so much being certain, it was easy to believe, with or without evidence, that they taught their pupils to disregard every duty but the pursuit of their own private advantage.

Protagoras. The first and most famous of the Sophists was Protagoras of Abdera. Born in the year 480 B.C., he became a paid teacher at thirty, and pursued that calling for a period of forty years with brilliant success, traversing the whole breadth of the Hellenic world, and, if we may judge from what seems to be the typical instance of Athens, exciting immense enthusiasm among the more enlightened classes of Greek society. Pericles debated moral problems with him, and he was employed to make laws for the Athenian colony of Thurii. On the occasion of a later visit to the imperial city public attention was drawn to the fact that Protagoras was a declared agnostic. A book of his began with the words: "As to the gods, I do not know whether they exist or not. Life is too short for such difficult inquiries." The author was expelled from Athens; a herald was sent round demanding the surrender of the book from all private individuals who possessed it; and the copies collected were burnt in the market-place. Protagoras himself was lost at sea on his way to Sicily. He was then nearly seventy. It may be that the treatise which gave occasion to such an outbreak of inquisitorial fanaticism had only just been written, and that the words about the shortness of life refer to the very limited time during which the author might expect his own intellectual activity to continue.

Humanism. Judging from the scanty materials at our disposal Protagoras was not only a great educator but also a great and original thinker. His profession of agnosticism must be read in company with another celebrated sentence quoted from the beginning of his work on Truth; "Man is the measure of all things, determining what does, and what does not, exist." Plato in his old age opposed to this the principle that God and not man is the true measure. That is to say, the standard of truth and good must be something ideal and beyond experience. And elsewhere he has tried to reduce the human test of reality to an absurdity by identifying it with the doctrine that when two people disagree they must both be right. It seems likely enough that Protagoras attached great importance to individual experience and conviction, to what we now call "the point of view." But, as Plato himself suggests, this was not inconsistent with discriminating between one person's opinion and another's with due regard to their respective authorities. And the Sophist's object would be to make his pupils better judges than they were before, the ultimate test of Tightness being reference to human interests rather than to the oracles of problematic gods.

While the standard varies from man to man, but with an appeal from the stupid and ignorant to the educated and intelligent, it also varies between ages and nations, involving a similar appeal from barbarism to civilization, from a less to a more advanced stage of social progress. Protagoras seems to have first discovered the doctrine of human development, viewing it as above all a moral growth. Perhaps the evolutionism of early Greek science suggested this view. According to a speech put into his mouth by Plato morality is the very foundation of human life, the condition of every other art, the essential distinction between brutes and men, between savages and civilized communities. Some are born with more, and some with less capacity for acquiring virtue; but that it is an acquisition is proved, among other ways, by the existence of penal law. For punishment can only be justified as a deterrent from wrong-doing- in other words as a moralizing agency. It would appear that the method followed by Protagoras as a teacher was quite in harmony with his Humanist philosophy. While the other Sophists gave young men the sort of scientific education that age afforded, i.e., a course of arithmetic, geometry, and astronomy, he took them straight to ethics and politics, interspersing his lectures with literary illustrations from the poets. According to him, the absolutely straight lines and perfect circles of geometry are fictions to which nothing in reality corresponds; nor do the celestial movements exhibit that exact uniformity assumed by the astronomers.

Hippias the Naturalist. That system of scientific education from which Protagoras so markedly separated himself found its most typical representative in Hippias of Elis. This very remarkable man seems to have originated the idea of natural law as the foundation of morality, distinguishing nature from the arbitrary conventions or fashions, differing according to the different times or regions in which they arise, imposed by arbitrary human enactment, and often unwillingly obeyed. He held that there is an element of right common to the laws of all countries and constituting their essential basis. He held also that the good and wise of all countries are naturally akin and should regard one another as citizens of a single state. This idea was subsequently developed by the Cynic and still more by the Stoic schools, passing from the latter to the jurists, in whose hands it became the great instrument for converting Roman law into a legislation for all mankind.

Hippias set a high value on truth as a virtue, preferring Achilles to Ulysses on account of his superior veracity. Perhaps it was as an exercise in pure truth that he inculcated the study of mathematics. And seeing how large a part equality plays in that study also, some Greeks cherished it as a lesson in justice. Euripides may have had the method of Hippias in view when he wrote the noble lines:

> "Honor Equality who binds together
> Both friends and cities and confederates;
> For equity is law, law equity,
> The lesser is the greater's enemy,
> And disadvantaged aye begins the strife.
> From her our measures, weights, and numbers come,
> Defined and ordered by Equality.
> So do the night's blind eye and sun's bright orb
> Walk equal courses in their yearly round,
> And neither is embittered by defeat."

Prodicus. We sometimes find the name of Prodicus associated with that of Hippias, as like him a somewhat younger contemporary of Protagoras. Both taught at Athens, and both seem to have represented the same naturalistic tendency of thought.

Plato, it is true, satirizes Prodicus as a rather pedantic lecturer on the niceties of language; but in this instance we probably get a juster idea of his importance from Aristophanes, who describes him as the most remarkable of the natural philosophers for wisdom and character, and who elsewhere playfully broaches a new theory of evolution which is to send Prodicus away howling. We also hear of this Sophist as having explained the origin of religion by the personification of natural objects; and Xenophon quotes a famous apologue of his, called "The Choice of Heracles," breathing the very spirit of naturalistic ethics. In particular it harmonizes admirably with the lines quoted above from Euripides, by showing that pleasure must either be purchased by toil or paid for by premature exhaustion.

Natural Law as the right of the Stronger. It will be remembered that Heracleitus brought the laws of the State into connection with the great cosmic law as the source whence their energy is derived. This idea was afterwards taken up and developed by the Stoics, who also adopted the physical philosophy of Heracleitus as the foundation of their system. Now, as the central precept of Stoicism is "follow Nature"- an obvious summary of what Hippias and Prodicus taught- we may legitimately regard these two Sophists as worthy successors in the ethical field to the great Ephesian master.

Their appeal to nature was not, however, to pass unchallenged. If, as seems more than possible, Protagoras first turned author in his later years, his proscription of physical studies and his theory of morality as a purely human product may well be interpreted as a criticism of the attempt made by his younger rivals to found morality on natural law, more especially as their ethical method was soon twisted, in a way that must have revolted them, into a justification of the claim put forward on behalf of the stronger, whether as states or as individuals, to plunder and destroy the weaker. Thucydides represents the Athenians as openly basing their foreign policy on the law of brute force; and it has been supposed that their cynical declarations in this respect, as well as the private demoralization described in their own literature, was the result of Sophistic teaching. Only since the last hundred years has it been made clear, chiefly by the labors of English scholars, that neither as humanists nor as naturalists can the Sophists be justly charged with any such corrupting influence. Their principles were liable to be misrepresented or misapplied, as are the principles of any philosophy, and, we may add, of any religion; but to no greater extent than has happened, for instance, with the lessons of their great opponent, Plato. On the whole, the new ideas they put in currency were distinctly a gain to Greece and to the world.

Gorgias the Anti-Naturalist. Gorgias of Leontini, a Sicilian teacher of rhetoric, counts among the great Sophists, while occupying a place somewhat apart from the three above considered. His principal contribution to philosophy, however, seems to associate him more nearly with Protagoras than with the naturalist couple. It is, in fact, a bold attempt to get rid of the idea of nature altogether by showing that there is no such thing. Gorgias conducts his campaign against objective reality in the paradoxical Greek style by establishing three propositions: (1) nothing is; (2) if anything existed it could not be known; (3) if it could be known the knowledge could not be communicated. For what contradicts itself cannot exist; and the philosophers have proved with equal cogency that nature is one and many, finite and infinite, with and without change. To be known, reality should be identified with thought, whereas some thoughts evidently represent nothing real. Nor can knowledge be communicated unless words are identified with the sensations they signify, which is not the fact.

As regards virtue, Gorgias taught that it is relative to the age and social position of the person concerned, a principle that reminds us of the short modern formula for conduct- "My station and its duties."

Abolitionism. It was quite in consonance with the humanist spirit that Agathon, a disciple of Gorgias, should make justice a result of mutual agreement among men rather than an image of mathematical equality; and that another of his disciples, Alcidamas, should call the laws "the bulwark of the city," and philosophy "the bulwark of the laws." Yet this reverence for human law, which all over the ancient world upheld slavery as a permanent social institution, did not prevent the same Alcidamas from declaring slavery illegitimate.

"God," according to him, "sent all men to be free; Nature made none a slave." That is the greatest, most pregnant word of Greek practical philosophy. Plato and Aristotle never got so far; Aristotle even explicitly denied that for one man to treat another as an animated tool was wrong. To accomplish so great an effort of thought it seems to have been necessary that the two principles which the two rival schools of Sophisticism had opposed to one another should be combined- that the ideal of nature should be recognized in the completed humanity of man.

CHAPTER V

SOCRATES

Personality. Socrates is the greatest name in the history of philosophy and at the same time its most popular, most familiar figure. J. A. Symonds tells us how the sight of a hemlock plant recalled the manner of his death to a Venetian gondolier. The charm of his personality is unique. We think of the Greek philosophers before and after him as of so many marble statues, but of him as a living, speaking human figure. Yet this figure is surrounded by a sort of mystery. It is still a question for what did he live and die. An enigma to his own age, he remains an enigma to us. If Plato may be trusted, he was even an enigma to himself. From that fame and that obscurity one fact at least emerges to begin with; the immense importance of the personal factor in his work, whatever the value of that work may turn out to be.

Sources of Information. Socrates himself never wrote a line about philosophy; and although numerous reports of his conversation have been preserved, it is doubtful whether any two consecutive sentences have been put down exactly as they were uttered. Nor can the numerous busts bearing his name be relied on as faithful copies of an original portrait. It is suspected that they merely reproduce the conventional mask of a Silenus mentioned by those who remembered him, as giving a good idea of the sage's unprepossessing features. We know that he was born about 469 B.C., and that by family and fortune he belonged to the poorer class of Athenian citizens, his father being a working sculptor and his mother a midwife. But the incidents of his early life are buried in deep obscurity. It would seem that he practiced his father's trade for a time and then abandoned it in order to devote himself exclusively to the cultivation of his own and of other people's intelligence.

Before the age of forty Socrates must have already gained a high reputation for wisdom, for we find the beautiful, gifted, and aristocratic Alcibiades frequenting his society as a fitting preparation for filling the highest political offices. Some ten years later Aristophanes, in his comedy *The Clouds*, already mentioned as a brilliant satire on the new culture, takes Socrates as a type of the whole Sophistic movement, an eager student of physical science, a dishonest atheist, and a corrupter of the youths who come to him for instruction.

Plato, writing long afterwards, puts into the mouth of Socrates an explicit repudiation of ever having been engaged in physical speculations, and in this respect he is fully borne out by the evidence of Xenophon, a fellow-disciple. We may take their word for it, without excluding the possibility that their master had gone into such studies enough to convince himself that for him at any rate they would be a waste of time. He was no less a genuine Athenian than Aristophanes; and except as a fashionable craze for a short period, physics never appealed to the Attic taste, nor did it owe at any time a single discovery to Attic genius. Like Protagoras, Socrates devoted himself to human interests, but unlike the great agnostic he shared the strong religious faith which nowhere had struck such deep roots as in Attic soil; and this faith stood high among the causes alienating him and his countrymen from the method of Hippias and Prodicus.

Not a Sophist. On the strength of his reputation as a teacher, Socrates was popularly classed among the Sophists. His intimate friends, however, justly insisted on the fundamental difference separating him from them. It consisted, to begin with, in the circumstance that the Sophists took pay and that he did not. Quite apart from the direct evidence of Plato and Xenophon, who only knew him late in life, we may gather as much from the satire of Aristophanes on his poverty-stricken appearance- a fact absolutely inconsistent with his making a trade of tuition.

The profession of Sophist was indeed considered more lucrative than honorable; and an Athenian citizen may well have considered it beneath his dignity to barter wisdom for gold, especially in the case of one's own countrymen, whom it seemed a sort of natural duty to help with advice. Protagoras and the others were strangers, with something of the discredit attaching to foreign adventurers about them. Socrates never left his native city except on military duty, which he performed as a heavy-armed foot soldier in three arduous campaigns, on one occasion saving the life of Alcibiades.

Irony. Supposing, however, that the position of the paid teacher at Athens had been not less dignified than that of a salaried professor among ourselves, still it was one that Socrates would have scrupled to assume. It would have been dishonest on his part to take money for teaching, because by his account he had nothing to teach. Our authorities are not agreed as to what was meant by this profession of universal ignorance- the Socratic irony, as it is called. Plato gives it a strong religious coloring. According to his story, an ardent admirer of Socrates, one Chaerephon, asked the oracle at Delphi was there any man wiser than he. The Pythian prophetess answered that there was no man wiser. Much surprised at being singled out for such a distinction, and conscious of not in the least deserving it, Socrates went about seeking for some one wiser than himself, but found none even among those whose reputation stood highest. For their pretended wisdom invariably broke down under his cross-examination; while at the same time he could not convince them that they knew no more than he did. Then at last the meaning of the oracle became plain. Wisdom belongs to the gods alone; no man knows anything, and he is wisest who has come to the consciousness of his own ignorance.

One is sorry to question such a beautiful story; but, like the Athenian celebrities, it breaks down under cross-examination. Socrates could not have got so great a reputation as is here presupposed without some more positive achievement than a general confession of ignorance; and as depicted by Xenophon, in this respect a much more trustworthy informant than Plato, it is only about natural philosophy that he professes to know nothing or to hold that nothing can be known, the causes of physical phenomena being, in his opinion, a secret that the gods have kept to themselves. On the other hand, the whole range of human interests lies open to man, and among the rest to himself.

The Dialectic Method. In limiting philosophy to the study of man, Socrates agrees with Protagoras, except that he approaches the subject from a religious rather than from an agnostic point of view. The distinctive originality of the Athenian thinker lies in his creation of a new method. Socrates figures in the history of philosophy before all things as the founder of logic, the first to attempt an organization of reason as such. Reasoning of course is as old as language, in a way it is as old as conscious life; the behavior of the most rudimentary animals is guided by their experience of the past. And long before Socrates the Greeks had learned to distinguish this power from all the lower manifestations of consciousness, to look on it as constituting their own superiority to the barbarians- the secret also of one man's superiority to another in the State. Then came philosophy, and raised reason to a higher pinnacle still as the cause alike of physical order and of civil law, the ruling power of the world. As such, Anaxagoras had introduced it to Athens under the name of Nous- the one Greek word still known to the most ignorant sporting man among ourselves. Another Greek word for reason, the one used by Heracleitus, is logos, whence comes our word logic, which means the science of reasoning, the analysis of its operations, the systematic exposition of the process by which conception, judgment, and inference, are successfully carried on.

Socrates did not create the science of logic- that was an achievement reserved for his successor, Aristotle- but without his pioneer work it could not have been created. How much he actually did we cannot tell with certainty, for Xenophon, to whom our most trustworthy information is due, had but a feeble hold on pure theory, and Plato's dramatic presentation of the old master gives such an immense extension to his method that the original nucleus cannot be isolated from subsequent accretions.

Definition. We know on the authority of Aristotle, confirmed by the detailed statements of Xenophon, that Socrates first introduced the methods of definition and induction. That is, he took some abstract term, by preference the name of a virtue or vice, such as Courage or Justice, Cowardice or Injustice, and by comparing together a number of concrete instances where those qualities were exhibited, sought to arrive at a general notion of what the word meant, of what we now call its connotation. According to him, such a procedure was necessary in order that discussions on subjects of general interest might be carried on in a friendly and profitable manner. And not only were definitions necessary in order that people might know what they were talking about, but the definitions themselves were to be arrived at as the result of a search jointly undertaken by the whole company, everybody present helping to the best of his ability in the hunt after truth. Socrates in fact applied the democratic tradition of Athens to scientific inquiry, not speaking with authority as the Sophists, but as professing to know no more than any one else; more concerned to ask questions than to answer them; always on the look-out for new facts and new ideas. His method reflected both the deliberations of the sovereign Assembly and the cross-examination to which defendants could subject their prosecutors in the popular law courts.

Of course Athens, even more than other Greek cities, abounded in persons having a good conceit of themselves; and pretenders to universal knowledge found a merciless critic in the poorly-dressed old man with the thick lips and flat, turned-up nose who, under the appearance of reverence for their superior wisdom and an insatiable thirst for information, by a series of searching questions speedily involved the pontifical charlatan in a mesh of hopeless self-contradiction. Such scenes no doubt suggested to Plato his imposing picture of Socrates as a divinely-commissioned prophet going about to convince the world of universal and hopeless ignorance, as prophets of another school go about to convince it of universal depravity. But the picture as it stands is not historical; and the real prophet had a message of reasoned truth rather than of reasoned nescience to deliver.

Division. More important even than Definition to clear thinking is the logical process of Division- the distribution of every subject discussed under a number of distinct headings. Descartes, the founder of modern French philosophy, mentions the plan of breaking up difficulties into the greatest possible number of parts as a first step to discovering their solution; and the same method was practiced by Socrates two thousand years before him. If, for instance, he were discussing the comparative claims of two rival statesmen to the name of a good citizen he would bring down the question to a specific estimate of their respective services in the various departments of political activity. A good citizen increases the resources of the State, defeats the enemy in war, wins allies by diplomacy, appeases intestine discords by his eloquence.

Reasoning. Definition and division are spoken of in logic as processes subsidiary to Inference- that is the discovery of new truths as necessary consequences of the truths we already know. Socrates was fully alive to this characteristic property of reasoning, and illustrated it in his conversations by starting from principles about which he and his interlocutor were agreed. Unfortunately Xenophon, on account of his very narrow range of interests, does not quote examples enough to show how Socrates habitually worked out his conclusions. But he gives us the valuable information that no man whom he ever knew was so successful in gaining the assent of his hearers- a fact quite inconsistent with Plato's account of his hero as an exasperating personage, reducing every one to shame if not to confession by his dialectical skill.

Final Causes. As it happens, the most celebrated instance of Socratic reasoning is one that modern science has shown to be much less convincing than used to be imagined. This is the well-known Theistic argument from design. As the structure of the human body exhibits an adaptation of means to ends such as we find in the works of skillful artificers, the existence of a powerful, intelligent, and benevolent Being is assumed as necessary to explain its origin. Whatever the argument may be worth, the credit of having discovered it clearly belongs to Socrates, for Anaxagoras, who comes nearest to him as a Theistic philosopher, conceived his Nous as working by mechanical impulse, not by design. And if there is any truth in the story of the oracle declaring him to be the wisest of men, we may suppose that it was due to the impression made on the Delphic authorities by his fame as the contributor of a new reason for believing in the gods at a time when philosophers in general passed for being atheists. As to the Socratic profession of ignorance, we are now in a better position to appreciate its value. It is a paradoxical way of saying that the logician as such need know nothing that commonly passes for knowledge.

By exposing the flaws in other people's theories he may prove that they are as ignorant as he is himself. Or again, by unfolding the implications of the facts supplied to him by other people, while securing their assent to every step in the chain of inference, he may make it seem as if the result obtained did as much credit to their wisdom as to his own. This is the method constantly followed by the Platonic Socrates, who in this respect may reproduce the spirit of the master more faithfully than Xenophon's photographic illustrations.

Socrates as a Moral Reformer. While Socrates interests us chiefly as the creator of logical method, the philosopher himself only valued that method as an instrument of moral reformation. As an Athenian citizen he took a profound personal interest in the good government of his country; and this patriotic motive was alone sufficient to distinguish him from the sophists, who as paid teachers and foreigners, could not be actuated by the same absorbing passion for the public good. At the same time it is clear that their comparative detachment and wide range of culture gave their ethical ideas a reach, an originality, and an emancipating power that his did not possess. The Humanism of Protagoras was pregnant with hopes of a higher civilization than. Greece had reached.

The Naturalism of Hippias and Prodicus embodied a reaction against perverted appetites from which Greece in less civilized ages had been free.

Utilitarianism. In accordance with the systematizing bent of his genius, Socrates seems to have sought for a single principle in ethics, and to have found it provisionally in the idea of utility; that is to say he introduced the method of estimating the morality of actions neither by public opinion nor by individual taste, but by their calculable consequences. We must not suppose, however, that his attempts in this direction amounted to an anticipation of utilitarianism in the modern sense.

As reported by Xenophon, he never commits himself to the assertion that pleasure and the absence of pain are the only desirable things. Nor, assuming that we have discovered in what utility consists- whether pleasurableness or anything else- does Socrates ever make it clear whether the conduct of the individual is to be determined by regard for his own advantage, or for the advantage of the community to which he belongs, or for that of the whole human race. That these respective claims might, apparently at least, collide was a difficulty first seriously discussed in all its bearings by Plato, who only hoped to solve it by revolutionizing public opinion, society, and religion. Socrates habitually appeals to self-interest, as if it were the only available motive; but he seems at the same time to be persuaded that the happiness of the citizen is in the long run identified with the happiness of the State. That, in fact, was not his question, but rather the question how an art of social life could be constructed comparable for systematic completeness to the industrial arts of which a city like Athens offered such multifarious examples.

The Lessons of Town Life. Aristophanes could not see the soul of Socrates, but he has taken a snapshot of the philosopher as he appeared to the man in the street, the accuracy of which is vouched for by Plato, "stalking about like a pelican and rolling his eyes." Nothing escaped those curious eyes, as nothing escaped Mr. Gladstone's, and their inquisitiveness found a rich harvest in a city where every calling was taught and practiced with complete publicity. Now what struck Socrates chiefly was the high value set on expert attainments, and the ready obedience given to professional trainers wherever a special technique had come to be recognized, as in the army and navy, the theater, the artist's studio, or the gymnasium, compared with the haphazard methods of politics, of the higher education, of social intimacies, of pleasure-seeking among the leisured classes. That any one should follow for his personal satisfaction a line of conduct which would not be tolerated for a day in the hired occupants of a responsible office, seemed to the philosopher a revolting paradox. Some may call this a bourgeois or Philistine morality. But what makes those names terms of reproach is their association with a slavish deference to custom and tradition. Socratic morality, by reducing life to a fine art, discards convention and opens possibilities of endless improvement.

Virtue as Knowledge. Greek philosophy delighted in paradoxes, and Socrates was credited with two such; first, the paradox of ignorance, which as we saw expressed in a picturesque way the discovery of fact by talking things over methodically, the evolution by logical processes of the unknown into the known; and secondly, the paradox, that virtue is identical with knowledge, so that he who has the right theory of conduct necessarily does what is right. Every one, said Socrates; does what he thinks is for his good; if he does wrong that only proves that he is mistaken in his belief and ought to be taught better. Such an idea is closely connected with the interpretation of morality as an art; the artist has in fact been defined as one who does his best. And it might be said that the man who scamps his work has mistaken beliefs about the good of making money or the good of saving time. The question ends by becoming a verbal one. If my friend tells me that he does what he knows is bad for him, and I observe that, if he really knew that, he would not do it, we are evidently not using the word "know" in the same sense. Or to put it somewhat differently, the Socratic philosophy which began as ultra -intellectualism ends in what would now be called ultra-pragmatism. Belief does not lead to practice; it is practice and nothing else.

The Divine Voice. Socrates did not succeed in reducing his own life to a work of art capable of being explained and justified as the expression of right theory in right practice. A place had to be left for the free play of unaccountable instincts or intuitions warning him without a reason that certain actions would have bad results. He interpreted these inward monitions as a divine voice accompanying him through life. By a misinterpretation which goes back to his own time this voice has often been described as a daemon or personal spirit. More recently it has been identified with conscience. But this view is inconsistent with the circumstance, mentioned by Plato, that the monitor always intervened to forbid, never to give a positive command. Conscience both forbids and commands; while in each instance its promptings can be referred to the known laws of moral obligation.

The Hero as a Philosopher. With Socrates himself to know the right and to do it were the same thing, and no doubt it was from a conviction that what was possible to him was equally possible to all men that he identified virtue with knowledge. For the unflinching performance of duty at all costs he is, so far as our information goes, without an equal in the ancient world. His services as a soldier in the field have been already mentioned. His conduct as a citizen at home is marked by still greater fortitude. It was his custom- at the bidding as he declared of the divine monitor- to abstain from all political activity. But there came a moment when a civic duty, accidentally imposed on the philosopher, showed of what mettle he was made.

Athens had won her last great victory over a Peloponnesian fleet at Arginusse. But to her people the victory became an occasion for mourning and indignation, because through the neglect, as was alleged, of the admirals a number of sailors had been left to perish in the waves, and what seemed still worse, the bodies of the dead were not picked up and brought home for burial. It was, therefore, resolved that the admirals who returned home, six in number, should be tried on this charge. So far no objection could be taken to the proceedings. The case was altered when the Senate accepted a resolution decreeing that the guilt or innocence of the accused parties should be submitted to a direct vote of the whole people instead of to a regular sworn jury, that they should not be heard in their own defense, and that their cases should be decided in a batch instead of being submitted one by one to the popular judgment, as was prescribed by law.

At first the Prytanes, a sort of municipal Board whose business it was to preside over the deliberations of the Sovereign Assembly, refused to commit the illegality of putting the question to the vote, but eventually all, with a single exception, yielded to the clamor of the multitude. That solitary representative of law and justice was Socrates, whom the chances of the lot had enrolled among the Prytanes of that day. His protest could not be overcome by threats of imprisonment and death, but being eventually passed over, it was powerless to save the unfortunate victors of Arginusse from condemnation and execution.

Two years after these events the democracy that had so abused its power was abolished by a foreign conqueror, and an oligarchy of thirty members imposed on Athens. These men soon inaugurated a reign of terror, killing and plundering to their heart's content. Within the city one voice alone was raised in fearless criticism of their insane violence, this time also the voice of Socrates. Critias, the leader of the terrorists, had been his pupil and was content to let the old philosopher off with a private warning to hold his tongue. Socrates also braved an insidious attempt of the thirty to make him an accomplice in their crimes. A certain Leon of Salamis, whose only offense was his wealth, had been marked out by them for proscription. Five citizens, of whom Socrates was one, received orders to arrest this man and bring him over to be executed. The other four went on the disgraceful errand; he remained at home.

Trial and Death of Socrates. It was reserved for the restored democracy to commit a crime from which even the cruel and unscrupulous oligarchs had recoiled. In the year 399 B.C. Socrates was prosecuted on a capital charge before the popular tribunal by Anytus, a democratic politician, Lycon, a public speaker, and Meletus, a poet. They accused him of denying the gods whom the State acknowledged, of introducing new gods whom the State did not acknowledge, and of being a corrupter of youth. In short, they represented the greatest and purest religious teacher Greece had ever seen of being an immoral and superstitious atheist. Athens, as has already been mentioned, was distinguished above all other Greek cities for intolerant bigotry. So far the victims of persecution had been philosophers whose ideas were irreconcilable with the current mythology, such as Anaxagoras and Protagoras, or who openly criticized it, such as Diagoras of Melos. But what makes the habit of punishing people for their opinions so peculiarly poisonous is that sooner or later it victimizes originality of every kind, even the originality that finds new arguments for old beliefs. Socrates incurred the suspicion of atheism simply because he met the atheists on their own ground, encountering reason with reason, and because he betrayed a thorough acquaintance with the theories he set himself to refute. To describe his divinely sent warnings as a newfangled religion was of course a misconception that a few words of explanation would dispel. A pamphleteer who renewed the attack on Socrates some years after his death supported the charge of corrupting youth by the examples of Alcibiades and Critias. Both had been his pupils, and both had turned out badly; but as Xenophon truly observes, whatever influence Socrates exercised over them was used to keep them straight, not to lead them astray.

Plato's account of his master's trial and death is a historical romance; but the main facts may be taken as faithfully related. The court which sat in judgment on Socrates consisted of 501 citizens chosen by lot. It seems to have made a bad impression on many of these persons that the old philosopher appealed to their reason instead of humbly throwing himself on their mercy, which in Xenophon's opinion would have insured his acquittal. Condemned by a small majority, and invited to propose a lighter penalty than the capital sentence demanded by his accuser, Socrates began by suggesting that maintenance at the public expense in the Prytaneum would be the proper recompense for the services he had rendered to the State. Then, waiving this claim as impracticable, he offered to pay a fine of thirty minae (about £122), as his friends would be willing to make up that much money among them. On a second vote the fearless old man was condemned to death, eighty of those who had pronounced him innocent now going over to the side of the majority.

It so happened that the condemnation fell at a time when, owing to the absence of a sacred mission sent to Delos, no capital sentence could be carried out at Athens. This gave a respite of thirty days to Socrates, who, had he chosen, might have profited by the delay to make his escape from prison. Everything had in fact been arranged for the purpose by his friends, but he refused to avail himself of their offers, on the ground that it would have involved disobedience to the laws. Accordingly on the expiration of the fatal term, after a last conversation with his followers, Socrates cheerfully met death in the way humanely prescribed at

Athens, by swallowing a draught of hemlock.

We owe it to the method and the example of this heroic sage, first, that philosophy has ever since centered in the study of mind rather than in the study of matter; and also that it has been understood to demand, so far as human frailty permits, a realization in its teachers' lives of the ideal that their moral theories set up. Hence the later schools of Greek philosophy, while more largely indebted to the Ionian cosmologists and to the Sophists than to Socrates for their speculative principles, exhibit in the character and attitude of their founders and chief representatives the unmistakable impress of his commanding personality.

EARLY GREEK PHILOSOPHY

WORKS BEARING ON EARLY GREEK PHILOSOPHY

Grote, *History of Greece*, chapters xvi., lxvii., and lxviii. *Plato*, chapters i. and ii.

Zeller, Ed., *Die Philosophie der Griechen*, Bd. i., 5te, Auflage (1892), and Bd. ii., 1. 4te Auflage, 1-232 (1889).

Tannery, Paul, *Pour l'Histoire de la Science Hellene* (1887).

Burnet, John, *Early Greek Philosophy* (1892).

Milhaud, Gaston, *La Science Grecque* (1893). *Les Philosophes Geometres de la Grece* (1900).

Gomperz, Th., *The Greek Thinkers*, vol. i. Translated by Laurie Magnus (1896).

Doring, A., *Die Lehre des Sokrates* (1896). *Geschichte der griechischen Philosophie*, i. 1-427 (1903).

Benn, A. W., *The Philosophy of Greece*, chapters i.-vi. (1898).

Piat, C, *Socrate* (1900).

Diels, H., *Fragmente der Vorsokratiker*, Band I. (1906).

THE END

Made in the USA
Columbia, SC
28 November 2023